AF539676

GUIDING STARS

A Sampler of Quilters' Favorite Quotations

Edited by Elaine Miles

Stars teach as well as shine.
— Edward Young

R. & E. Miles
*San Pedro * 1989*

Library of Congress Catalog Number: 88-092035
ISBN: 0-936810-14-9
Manufactured in the U.S.A.
92 91 90 89 4 3 2 1

We have received permission from many publishers and authors to reprint their copyrighted material. These permissions will be found in Acknowledgements, beginning on page 263.

Type set by Mary Meyer, Entropy Enterprises, San Pedro, California
Printed on acid-free paper and bound by Thompson-Shore, Inc., Dexter, Michigan

The quilt block which comprises the overall pattern design of the cover is *Guiding Stars*.

Peace and Plenty

R. & E. Miles
Post Office Box 1916
San Pedro, California 90733
(213) 833-8856

For my parents,
whose guiding stars
still show the way.

Contents

Preface

> I pluck up the goodlisome herbs of sentences by pruning, eat them by reading, digest them by musing, and lay them up at length in the high seat of memory by gathering them together; that so, having tasted their sweetness, I may the less perceive the bitterness of life.
>
> Queen Elizabeth I

Although Queen Elizabeth and I probably do not have many other things in common, we both in our lifetimes have been collectors of quotations, and for essentially the same reasons. Life, whether lived in a 16th century castle or a 20th century California cottage, has its inevitable difficulties, and there are times when we lose not only heart but perspective and need the support of someone else's wisdom and experience.

Blessings on the gift of language that allows each of us to enjoy this support. For without the word we would be isolated within our frail mortalities, our knowledge limited to the narrow span of a human lifetime. There would be neither news from the past nor messages for the future. No Bible. No Shakespeare. No Grandmother's Favorite.

Since childhood, reading has been one of my greatest pleasures and I too have gathered up my own private collection of "goodlisome herbs." What a comforting sense of kinship to meet in the lines of poem or paragraph another person saying some of the very things I have thought or felt. Reaching across time and space to open a door, turn on a light, offer a steadying hand, give a push, or tickle a funny bone. Suddenly with a "letter" from another traveler to act as guidebook, map, manual or "rest-stop" diversion, the beautiful and awful journey seems less lonely.

This particular collection of "letters" had its beginnings in a $3.95 treasure from a used book store and the comment of a friend. *The Desk Drawer Anthology: Poems for the American People* (1937, Doubleday, Doran) compiled and edited by Theodore Roosevelt, Jr. and Alice Roosevelt Longworth, is a gathering of favorite verse, cut from newspapers and magazines and sent to the Roosevelts from across the United States over 50 years ago. When I mentioned the book at lunch one day, Odette Teel said, "I bet quilters have a lot of good poems put away in their desk drawers, too." Her remark started me thinking about a variation on *The Desk Drawer Anthology*.

All of us are part of several worlds, the common one we share with life and the planet, and then those others whose boundaries are set by family, place, livelihood, and interests. We participate in, and know, parts of the larger world, but it is within the smaller worlds that most real life is lived.

Since 1973, one of my small worlds has been that of quilting. Odette's observation made me aware of the wonderful opportunity for combining a love of quilts with a love of quotations — as well as satisfying an insatiable curiosity about other people's sources of comfort, cheer, and inspiration (not to mention the chance to send my own favorites out into the world).

The 139 contributors to this book have been

involved in quilting in some way during the past 20 years and their work in its myriad forms has enriched my own quilting life. No world can be completely encompassed, but quilting's nets spread wide and deep, and this sample of practitioners and devotees gives an idea of its diversity, and in this diversity a reflection of the larger world.

The words have come from quilters, but the messages are universal, addressing the traveler in all of us. I hope each reader will find something new within these pages to lay up in their own "high seat of memory" for sweetening the journey.

SAN PEDRO, CALIFORNIA ELAINE MILES
FEBRUARY 1989

Notes on the Quotations

The contributor of the quotation is to the left.

The author of the quotation, along with the work from which it is taken, and the date (if it could be found) when the words were first published or said, is to the right. A parenthetical note appearing here indicates a comment by the contributor.

Quotations without a contributor's name were chosen by the editor.

Within the text, the contributor's own words are italicized. If unattributed, italicized words are the editor's.

Any quotation credited to "Author unknown" means that after exhausting my research resources the author remained unknown to me. If any reader has additional information about these quotations I would be happy to hear from them.

Someone, himself an author unknown, said, "If it is the truth, what does it matter who said it?" In bringing this anthology together, I have found that it does indeed matter very much, especially to the copyright holder, not only *who* said it, but *how* it was said. In the case of *how*, every effort has been made to present the quotation as I felt the author intended. In a few instances, after checking and deliberating, some slight changes in the material as the contributor sent it were made. This happened most often in the punctuation, capitalization and line-lengths of poetry. A delicate balance of responsibility to contributor, author, and book was involved, with final advantage going to the author.

All Bible quotations unless otherwise stated are from the King James Version.

Classic quilt patches serve as category headings rather than the more usual "Ambition, Integrity, Piety, and Zeal." The result is, perhaps, a little different way of looking at the quotations. If one occasionally seems out of place, hopefully the reader will agree that such things are finally a matter of personal interpretation. The editor did strive for "sense" as much as "sensibility." And if a quilt patch appears familiar to you but the name seems wrong, it must be kept in mind that of the hundreds of quilt block designs many not only have more than one name, but often the same name will apply to different patches.

The preponderance of the masculine pronoun in the quotations was pointed out by the copy editor, a perceptive young man. He is correct, of course, but being of my time and place, I have grown used to the generic "he," and find alterations too often make for awkward reading. In tribute to my upbringing, it never occurred to me, either in childhood or now, that I wasn't included too.

Guiding Stars, with its approximately 650 entries, is a comparatively small anthology. It is hoped readers will see this as a benefit, allowing them to become familiar with the book in its entirety, making it an agreeable, sustaining companion both for the night-side table and the traveling bag.

Notes on the Biographies

Knowing something of the people responsible for a book gives it a framework and reality it would not otherwise have. In the case of *Guiding Stars,* with its 139 contributors, the biographies are, of necessity, brief and not intended as a complete listing of achievements, but rather meant to give an idea of where that person fits in the many-faceted world of quilting.

The authors' biographies are even briefer, basically supplying dates, nationality, and profession, the premise being that further information is available at the library. A work, sometimes two, is included when such is inextricably connected with the person, or to serve as a further guide, but is no measure of the person's lifetime achievements. Sometimes, I found a fact particularly interesting or revealing, so included it. For a few people, I could find nothing at all.

GUIDING STARS

Angel's Trumpet

Be not forgetful to entertain strangers: for thereby some have entertained angels unawares.

NORMA BRADLEY ALLEN — Hebrews 13:2

> The humble worker do not scorn,
> He could be president on the morn.

JOSEPH F. HOLLINGSHEAD — Folk rhyme

The measure of a man's real character is what he would do if he knew he would never be found out.

JUDY REHMEL — Thomas Babington Macaulay

There is no limit to what can be accomplished so long as it does not matter who gets the credit.

KAREY BRESENHAN
IÒNE McINTYRE — Miguel de Cervantes, c. 1615

So Peter rose and went with them. And when he had come, they took him to the upper room. All the widows stood beside him weeping, and showing tunics and other garments which Dorcas made while she was still with them.

Acts 9:39
Revised Standard
Version

Moral: Beware lest the quilt tasks and unregarded craftspersons disappear from our world. They may be too valuable for our lives to do without. Machines do nothing just for love and beauty.

DOLORES A. HINSON

My Soul goes clad in gorgeous things,
Scarlet and gold and blue,
And at her shoulder sudden wings
Like long flames flicker through.
. . . .
O folk who scorn my stiff gray gown,
My dull and foolish face,
Can ye not see my Soul flash down,
A singing flame through space?

EMILY J. WALDEN

Fannie Stearns Davis
"Souls"

Take heed of still waters, they quick pass away.

SHEILA M. GROMAN

George Herbert
Jacula Prudentum,
1651

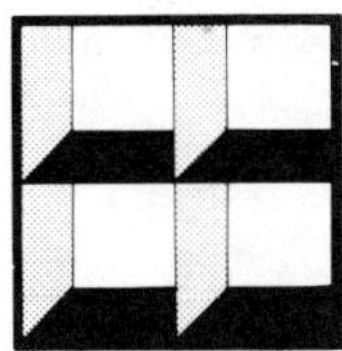

Attic Window

A mind, like a window, should always be kept open, at least a crack, to allow for the circulation of some fresh air.

Elaine Miles

The privilege of a human being is to change.

JOAN SCHULZE

Jeanne Moreau
quoted in "*W*"
Magazine,
October 1985

A foolish consistency is the hobgoblin of little minds . . .

NANCY HALPERN

Ralph Waldo Emerson
"Self Reliance," 1841

Never assume.

JUDY ROBBINS

Author unknown

A grace to pray for — that our self-interest, which is inescapable, shall never cripple our sense of humor, that fully conscious self-scrutiny which alone can save us.

DIXIE HAYWOOD

Dag Hammarskjold
Markings, 1964

When one does not have the necessary power, one has to adjust his ego.

U KHIN

Burmese proverb

Originality: an uncommon response to a problem.

JOHN MANGIAPANE

Jean Ray Laury

The foolish and the dead alone never change their opinions.

EMILY J. WALDEN

James Russell Lowell
My Study Windows, 1871

If you always do what you've always done, you'll always get what you've always gotten.

JEANNIE M. SPEARS

From a neurolinguistic programming workshop

If you can't change, you're gonna die.

DIANN LOGAN

Bob Dylan

There is no sin except stupidity.

PATRICIA J. MORRIS

Oscar Wilde
The Critic as Artist,
1891

No matter how far you have gone on a wrong road, turn back.

THERESA MILLETT

Turkish proverb

Beacon Lights

Books are lighthouses erected in the great sea of time.

Henry Benjamin Whipple

The habit of reading lasts when all other pleasures fade. It will make your hours pleasant to you as long as you live.

LOUISE O. TOWNSEND — Anthony Trollope

When I get a little money, I buy books; and if any is left, I buy food and clothes.

SHIRLEY CONLON — Desiderius Erasmus

In the highest civilization, the book is still the highest delight. He who has once known its satisfactions is provided with a resource against calamity.

THERESA MILLETT — Ralph Waldo Emerson

There is no Frigate like a Book
To take us Lands away
Nor any Coursers like a Page
of prancing Poetry —
This Traverse may the poorest take
Without oppress of Toll —
How frugal is the chariot
That bears the Human soul.

DOROTHY COZART — Emily Dickinson, c. 1873

How many a person has dated a new era in his life from the reading of a book?

BLANCHE L. CONNOLLY — Henry David Thoreau *Walden*, 1854

The man who does not read good books has no advantage over the man who can't read them.

LOUISE O. TOWNSEND — Mark Twain

Heaven must be a place of endless bookshelves, never quite filled with books, and always with room for one more.

SHIRLEY CONLON — Franklin Mason

I guard the fragrance of a thousand springs.
Draw near! draw near!
Ten thousand yesterdays are gathered here.

EMILY J. WALDEN

Yuan Mei
"In an Old Library,"
c. 1760

A man, in his books, may be said to walk the earth a long time after he is gone.

LOUISE O. TOWNSEND

John Muir

You think your pain and heartbreak are unprecedented in the history of the world, but then you read. It was books that taught me that the things that tormented me most were the very things that connected me with all the people who were alive, or have ever been alive.

ELAINE MILES

James Baldwin as quoted in *Books and the Teen-age Reader* by G. Robert Carlson, 1967

Blazing Star

Climb high
Climb far
Your goal the sky
Your aim the star.

LaVONNE R. HANLON

Inscription on Hopkins Memorial Steps, Williams College, Williamstown, Massachusetts

Ah, but a man's reach should exceed his grasp,
Or what's a heaven for?

JANE BLAIR
PAULA LEDERKRAMER
PATRICIA J. MORRIS

Robert Browning
"Andrea del Sarto,"
1855

You can do anything if you have enthusiasm. It is the yeast that makes your hopes rise to the stars.

KAREN BRAY

Henry Ford

Nothing great was ever achieved without enthusiasm.

MARGARET M. CAVIGGA

Ralph Waldo Emerson
"Civilization," 1870

sleep leads to dreaming
waking to imagination and to
imagine what we
could be, o,
what we could be.

GENEVIEVE P. GURACAR

Susan Griffin
"To Gather
Ourselves," 1973

She who says it can't be done is interrupted by she who is doing it.

JOYCE SCHLOTZHAUER

Found in a Chinese
fortune cookie (and
yes, it had the
feminine pronoun)

Good, better, best —
never let it rest
    Till good is better
and better's best.

LAHOMA BUTLER RACKLEY

Quoted by my mother,
Stella Johnson Butler

Nothing in the world can take the place of persistence. Talent will not; nothing is more common than unsuccessful men with talent. Genius will not; unrewarded genius is almost a proverb. Education alone will not; the world is full of educated derelicts. Persistence and determination alone are omnipotent.

LINDA OTTO LIPSETT — Calvin Coolidge

Life is not a "brief candle." It is a splendid torch that I want to make burn as brightly as possible before handing it on to future generations.

LOIS K. IDE — George Bernard Shaw

I learned this at least from my experiment: that if one advances confidently in the direction of his dreams, and endeavors to live the life which he has imagined, he will meet with a success unexpected in common hours.

JUDY ROBBINS — Henry David Thoreau
Walden, 1854

The only thing that is not chance is what one asks of oneself and how well or badly one meets one's own standards.

SUELLEN MEYER — May Sarton
Journal of a Solitude, 1973

Until one is committed, there is hesitancy, the chance to draw back, always ineffectiveness, concerning all acts of initiative (and creation). There is one elementary truth the ignorance of which kills countless ideas and splendid plans: that the moment one definitely commits oneself, then Providence moves too. All sorts of things occur to help one that would never otherwise have occurred. A whole stream of events issues from the decision, raising in one's favor all manner of unforeseen incidents and meetings and material assistance which no man could have dreamed would have come his way. Whatever you can do or dream you can, begin it. Boldness has genius, power and magic in it. Begin it now.

MARGARET J. MILLER
JOYCE SCHLOTZHAUER

Johann Wolfgang von Goethe

To achieve all that is possible we must attempt the impossible — to be as much as we can be, we must dream of being more.

PATRICIA COX

Gale Baker Stanton

Here lies Jack Williams. He done his damnedest.

ELAINE MILES

An epitaph in the cemetery at Tombstone, Arizona

"I think I can, I think I can, I think I can . . . ."

Watty Piper, 1961

My mother often read to me when I was a child, and a favorite story was The Little Engine That Could. *She could always calm my temper, if some challenge frustrated me, by reciting the little engine's words, so that, still today, when I feel "stuck" or overwhelmed, I can hear her voice imitating the little huffing-puffing train.*

DIANN LOGAN

. . . I have had a chance to observe people at the top of just about every field. And it makes no difference if they are male or female, black or white, old or young, the people I observed succeeding are those who have been taught, or who teach themselves, to strive for excellence. The pleasure comes from knowing you have done a job the best way you know how. It seems to me, however, in our modern society that there is very little done these days in pursuit of excellence. But whatever there is, it stands out for its rarity.

JUDY FLORENCE

Jessica Savitch
from an interview

Hitch your wagon to a star.

MARGARET M. CAVIGGA

Ralph Waldo Emerson
"Circles," 1841

Bluebirds Flying

"Hope" is the thing with feathers —
That perches in the soul —
And sings the tune without the words —
And never stops — at all —

Emily Dickinson,
c. 1861

You cannot prevent the birds of sadness from flying over your head, but you can prevent them from nesting in your hair.

JUDY REHMEL — Chinese proverb

When cheerfulness is kept up on principle, against all odds, it is the finest form of courage.

FLAVIN GLOVER — Oridio Michel Magri

Our greatest glory consists not in never falling, but in rising every time we fall.

CARLA HASSEL — Oliver Goldsmith

Pain and suffering are inevitable — misery is optional. Joy continues to be my choice.

JUDY S. TOMLONSON — Penny Mossman, a victim of Hodgkin's disease who died in the spring of 1986

If we have risen with Christ, then we must dare to stand by him in the loneliness of his passion.

JEAN EITEL — Thomas Merton

Always do what you are afraid to do.

MARGARET HORTON — Ralph Waldo Emerson

If you keep a green bough in your heart, the singing bird will come.

JOANNE KOST — Chinese proverb

Brave World

O brave new world,
That has such people in't!

William Shakespeare
The Tempest, 1611

When the bells of peace ring, there will be no hand to beat the drums of war.

LOUISE O. TOWNSEND

Anwar Sadat, c. 1977

When that time comes when love is no more bought or sold, when it is not a means of making bread, when each woman's life is filled with earnest independent labor, then love will come to her, a strange and sudden sweetness breaking in upon her earnest work; not sought for, but found.

MARINA SALUME

Olive Schreiner
The Story of an African Farm, 1883

Let us not wallow in the valley of despair. I say to you today, my friends, even though we face the difficulties of today and tomorrow, I still have a dream. It is a dream deeply rooted in the American dream that one day this nation will rise up and live out the true meaning of its creed — we hold these truths to be self-evident, that all men are created equal . . . .

"From every mountainside, let freedom ring." . . . And when we allow freedom to ring, when we let it ring from every village and hamlet, from every state and city, we will be able to speed up that day when all of God's children — black men and white men, Jews and Gentiles, Catholics and Protestants, will be able to join hands and sing in the words of the old Negro spiritual, "Free at last! Free at last! Thank God almighty, we are free at last!"

DIANN LOGAN

Martin Luther King, Jr.
Keynote Address to the March on Washington, D.C., for Civil Rights,
August 28, 1963

The great aim of culture [is] the aim of setting ourselves to ascertain what perfection is and make it prevail.

PATRICIA J. MORRIS

Matthew Arnold
Culture and Anarchy,
1869

Do not waste your Time with the lies of Politicians. There is no such thing as military Power, only military Terrorism. The only True Power is the Sun, the Wind, the Tornadoes. We have that Potential for Power. We are a natural part of the earth. We must not allow them to smash us. This is our Obligation to the Earth.

GENEVIEVE P. GURACAR

John Trudell, Native American poet and teacher

We must learn to use our world sparingly and with tenderness . . . .

ELAINE MILES

Carlos Castaneda

I get up in the morning and watch the sunrise, and it smacks the nighttime and cleans out the sky and never makes a sound. And I know that's the God force. There's no Russian or American military might, nothing Hitler and the Nazis ever put together, that could make the nighttime disappear.

Once you get clear spiritually it's gonna clear up everything you do. You shoot dice better. You see color better. Your reasoning gets better. And then a lot of old petty things that you get hung up with, you don't anymore.

JUDY ROBBINS

Dick Gregory

The next war will determine not what is right but what is left.

MARY SCHAFER

Author unknown

Let us join together throughout the world to grow more food, to heal and prevent disease, to conserve and develop the resources of the good earth to the glory of God and the comfort of man's distress.

BLANCHE L. CONNOLLY

Society of Friends
"Declaration," World Conference, Oxford, England, 1952, in commemoration of their 300th anniversary

For wherefore is it that there is such wars and rumors of wars in the nations of the earth? And wherefore are men so mad to destroy one another? But only to uphold civil property . . . .

THERESA MILLETT

Gerrard Winstanley
The True Levellers' Standard Advanced, 1649

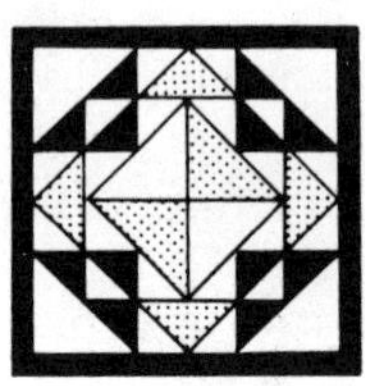

Corn and Beans

God gives the grain, but we must make the furrow.

Bohemian proverb

The Lord helps them that help themselves.

JOYCE GROSS

Proverb

You cannot teach a man anything.
You can only help him discover it within himself.

GWEN MARSTON

Galileo Galilei

Amateurs hope. Professionals work.

PATRICIA J. MORRIS

Garson Kanin

If you don't know what you need, no one is going to be able to help you find it.

JOHN MANGIAPANE

Jeannie M. Spears
The Professional Quilter, July 1984

If you think you can, or if you think you can't — you're right.

CINDY V. DAVIS — Author unknown

If you believe in it, fight for it. Anything worthwhile does not come easy.

MILLIE LEATHERS — A "Golden Rule" used in the rearing of my three children

We are faced with a series of great opportunities brilliantly disguised as impossible situations.

RODERICK KIRACOFE — Author unknown
My mother has carried this in her wallet for years.

The trouble with opportunity is that it always comes disguised as hard work.

JUDY REHMEL — Author unknown

Some people pray for more than they are willing to work for.

LOIS K. IDE — Author unknown

Delectable Mountains

More than a hundred years ago a woman lived in New Jersey, poor, sick, bedridden. Her solace was one book, *Pilgrim's Progress.* No doubt it eased her to think of the pilgrims who escaped from Doubting Castle and Giant Despair and "came to the Delectable Mountains — behold the gardens and orchards, the vineyards and fountains of water."

She made a patchwork pattern of pointed oblongs, clear red on white; she set the bright peaks around square beyond square in ranges that keep the eye climbing upward as mountains do. She named it The Delectable Mountains, and it is an outburst of joy. Only this quilt itself can give its effect. At the sight of it, every face brightens.

How can a few notes of music, some paint on canvas, mere pieces of cloth sewed together, have this power to lift the human spirit? No one can explain this; it is the mystery of art.

HELEN M. ERICSON

Rose Wilder Lane
Woman's Day Book of American Needlework, 1963

A thing of beauty is a joy forever:
Its loveliness increases; it will never
Pass into nothingness. . . .

MARGARET M. CAVIGGA
DORIS L. SCOTT

John Keats
"Endymion," 1818

It was filled with the most beautiful quilts. I got to the one that had won the blue ribbon and all the hairs on my body stood up. I was awe-struck. It was a quilt made by a lady who had used all of the ribbons — red, blue and white — that she had won all her life. It was the size of a double bed. It was not only beautiful, it was her history. It showed such care and sweet labors. I just hope we artists live up to that.

MARGIT ECHOLS

Lee Friedlander, photographer, upon receiving the MacDowell Colony award for lifetime achievement in the arts, August 17, 1986

Color speaks all languages.

LOIS K. IDE

Joseph Addison

An artist is not a special kind of person. Every person is a special kind of artist.

JINNY BEYER

Eric Gill

Life has loveliness to sell,
  All beautiful and splendid things,
Blue waves whitened on a cliff,
  Soaring fire that sways and sings,
And children's faces looking up
Holding wonder like a cup.

JEAN DUBOIS

Sara Teasdale
"Barter,"
Poetry Magazine,
1917

Dove of Peace

Lord,
  make me an instrument of Your peace.
  Where there is hatred let me sow love;
  Where there is injury, pardon;
  Where there is doubt, faith;
  Where there is despair, hope;
  Where there is darkness, light; and
  Where there is sadness, joy.
O divine Master,
grant that I may not so much
  Seek to be consoled as to console;
  To be understood as to understand;
  To be loved as to love;
  For it is in giving that we receive;
  It is in pardoning that we are pardoned; and
  It is in dying that we are born to eternal life.

BETH GUTCHEON

St. Francis of Assisi,
1181–1226

Lord, Thou knowest better than I know myself that I am growing older, and will some day be old.

Keep me from getting talkative, and particularly the fatal habit of thinking I must say something on every subject and on every occasion. Release me from the craving to try to straighten out everyone's affairs. Keep my mind free from the recital of endless details — give me wings to get to the point.

I ask for grace enough to listen to the tales of others' pains. Help me to endure them with patience.

But seal my lips on my own aches and pains — they are increasing and my love of rehearsing them becomes sweeter as the years go by.

Teach me the glorious lesson that occasionally it is possible that I may be mistaken.

Keep me reasonably sweet; I do not want to be a saint — some of them are so hard to live with — but a sour old person is one of the crowning works of the devil.

Make me thoughtful, but not moody; helpful, but not bossy. With my vast store of wisdom, it seems a pity not to use it all, but Thou knowest, Lord, that I want a few friends at the end.

ELAINE MILES

"A Mother Superior's Prayer" (The author is unknown to me, but my mother-in-law, Verna Phillips Miles, had this prayer taped on her refrigerator door the last years of her life.)

God grant me the Serenity to accept the things I cannot change.
The Courage to change those that I can.
And the Wisdom to know the difference.

Reinhold Niebuhr
"Prayer," 1934

MILLIE LEATHERS
JESSIE MacDONALD
JULIA A. NEEDHAM

Economy

Our life is frittered away by detail . . . Simplify, simplify.

KAREN BRAY

Henry David Thoreau
Walden, 1854

Necessity is the mother of invention.

SARAH HASS

Ancient anonymous
Latin saying

If you think education is expensive, you ought to try ignorance.

LOIS K. IDE
MARY SCHAFER

Derek Bok

Less is more.
God is in the details.

ELAINE MILES

Ludwig Mies van der Rohe

Where, oh where does the garbage go,
After it leaves the pail?
Where, oh where does the garbage go,
Does it go out in the mail?

Sadie, Mabel and
Gertrude Gallivan
"Song," 1955

If our world is not to become one great trash-heap we must learn to "use it up, wear it out, do without," instead of throwing things away — for there is no "away."

THERESA MILLETT

Frugality is not the point. Nor waste.
It's just that very little is discarded
in any honest spending of the self,
and what remains is used and used
again, worn thin by use, softened
to the pliancy and the translucence
of old linen, patched, mended, reinforced,
and saved . . . .

Robin Morgan
"Piecing," 1978

SARAH HASS

End of the Day

Now the day is over
　Night is drawing nigh;
Shadows of the evening
　Steal across the sky.

Sabine Baring-Gould
"Now the Day Is
Over," 1865

"I made every stitch o' that spread before me and Abram was married," she said. "I put it on my bed when we went to housekeepin'; it was on the bed when Abram died and when I die I want 'em to cover me with it." There was a life history in the simple words.

HELEN M. ERICSON

Eliza Calvert Hall
Aunt Jane of
Kentucky, 1907

So we die before our own eyes; so we see some chapters of our lives come to their natural end.

THERESA MILLETT

Sarah Orne Jewett
The Country of the Pointed Firs, 1896

We've known so much of happiness
We've had our cup of joy,
And memory is one gift of God
that death cannot destroy.

LaVONNE R. HANLON

Albert Kennedy Rosewell
"Should You Go First," 1948

I knew quite well that some day
I must go down this road;
but I had never thought
that some day would be today.

EMILY J. WALDEN

Narihara, c. 870 A.D.

God made memories so that we might have roses in December.

DOROTHY BETTIS

From a greeting card

Presentiment — is that Long Shadow — on the
Lawn —
Indicative that Suns go down —

The Notice to the startled Grass
That Darkness — is about to pass —

ELAINE MILES — Emily Dickinson, 1863

As a day well spent brings happy sleep, so a life spent well brings happy death.

LOUISE O. TOWNSEND — Leonardo da Vinci, c. 1500

Garden of Eden

And the Lord God planted a garden eastward in Eden; and there he put the man whom he had formed.

Genesis 2:8

What was Paradise? but a garden,
an orchard of trees and herbs,
full of pleasure, and nothing there but delights.

MARINA SALUME

William Lawson
A New Orchard and Garden, 1618

An old garden is like an old life. Who plants from youth to age writes a record of the years in leaf and blossom.

EMILY J. WALDEN

Eliza Calvert Hall
Aunt Jane of Kentucky, 1907

God gave all men all earth to love,
but since our hearts are small
ordained for each one spot should prove
beloved over all.

MARINA SALUME — Rudyard Kipling

Where is Heaven? Is it not
Just a friendly garden plot,
Walled with stone and roofed with sun,
Where the days pass one by one
Not too fast and not too slow,
Looking backward as they go . . .

BLANCHE L. CONNOLLY — Bliss Carman
"Where Is Heaven?"

Up the barley rows,
stitching, stitching them together,
a butterfly goes.

MARINA SALUME — Sora

Good Cheer

What an ornament and safeguard is humor . . . . It is a genius itself, and so defends from the insanities.

Sir Walter Scott

"How do you feel?"
"Well, I feel fine, if you don't ask for details."

LOUISE O. TOWNSEND

Katharine Hepburn,
from an interview

To live to be a hundred is no wish of mine — but I'm not sure it won't be when I'm ninety-nine.

LOIS K. IDE

Ida M. Pardue

I don't play accurately—anyone can play accurately—but I play with wonderful expression.

JANET B. ELWIN

Oscar Wilde
The Importance of Being Earnest, 1895

We can't all be heroes because someone has to sit on the curb and clap as they go by.

HAZEL CARTER

Will Rogers

The years between 50 and 70 are the hardest. People keep asking you to do things and you're not decrepit enough to refuse.

DOROTHY COZART

T.S. Eliot

Everyone is entitled to my opinion.

MILDRED L. MORGON

Author unknown
On a sign embroidered
for me by a friend

"Well!" said Miss Pole sitting down with the decision of a person who has made up her mind as to the nature of life and the world . . . "men will be men. Every mother's son of them wishes to be considered Samson and Solomon rolled into one — too strong ever to be beaten or discomfited — too wise ever to be outwitted. . . . My father was a man, and I know the sex pretty well."

BLANCHE L. CONNOLLY

Mrs. Gaskell
Cranford, 1853

Thinking the world should entertain you leads to boredom and sloth. Thinking you should entertain the world leads to bright clothes, odd graffiti and amazing grace in running for the bus.

JOAN SCHULZE

Anne Herbert
The Rising Sun Neighborhood Newsletter, quoted in *The Next Whole Earth Catalogue*, 1980

No man is fast enough to keep up with his good intentions.

JUDY REHMEL

The Lutheran Digest

Be grateful for the luck. Pay the thunder no mind—listen to the birds. And don't hate nobody.

LOUISE O. TOWNSEND

Eubie Blake at 100, c. 1983

If you cannot be a golden pippin, don't turn crabapple.

KAREY BRESENHAN

Pieties quilt, collection of the Museum of American Folk Art

If you can't get 5, take 2.

JEFFREY GUTCHEON — Milton Brown and The Texas Brownies

Well, thee knows it takes a mighty good husband to be better than none.

EMILY J. WALDEN — Elderly Quaker woman, 19th century

Some people think it's difficult to be a Christian and to laugh, but I think it's the other way around. God writes a lot of comedy — it's just that he has so many bad actors.

JUDY S. TOMLONSON — Garrison Keillor Address, Goshen College, 1986

The hurrier I go, the behinder I get.

JUDY REHMEL — Pennsylvania Dutch saying

The older I get, the behinder I get.

BONNIE LEONARD

On an occasion of this kind it becomes more than a moral duty to speak one's mind. It becomes a pleasure!

PATRICIA J. MORRIS

Oscar Wilde
The Importance of Being Earnest, 1895

God grant me the patience to endure my blessings — NOW.

SHARYN CRAIG

Author unknown

I have heard with admiring submission the experience of the lady who declared that the sense of being perfectly well-dressed gives a feeling of inward tranquility which religion is powerless to bestow.

ELAINE MILES

Ralph Waldo Emerson
"Social Aims," 1876

Too many cooks in the pot spoils the broth.

JEAN RAY LAURY

Quoted by an old neighbor

The compulsion for me to get my cotton-pickin' fingers on my fellow man is the natural result of my belief that I have the *word.* If I do have the word and feel surrounded by unmolded clay, I have no choice but to mold. When I do this, I begin playing God, and as a result usually raise the devil.

SUSAN K. TURBAK

G.A. Young, an Omaha psychiatrist, quoted in *A Circle of Quiet* by Madeleine L'Engle, 1972

The most completely lost of all days is that on which one has not laughed.

JUDY REHMEL
LOUISE O. TOWNSEND

Sebastien R.N. Chamfort, *Maxims and Thoughts*, 1796

Grandmother's Favorite

In fact, nothing has been said that has not been said before.

Terence
Eunuchus, 2nd
century B.C.

. . . short sentences drawn from long experiences.

Miguel de Cervantes,
c. 1615

In this section we have a sampling of proverbs, sayings, and teachings that have given generations of people encouragement, inspiration, example, and impetus. Since this wisdom is usually passed on orally, the "author" of each quotation is listed (when such is the case) as the person from whom the contributor first heard the words (where there are multiple contributors the name of any "authors" appears on the same line as the specific contributor). Each quotation is followed by ancestor or companion quotes as an example of how the words may change but the thoughts remain basic, universal, and human through time and place.

Let us begin with the most universal and basic law of all, the Golden Rule:

Do unto others as you would have them do unto you.

VIRGINIA AVERY — A constant admonition of my mother's

IRENE GOODRICH — My mother

Deal with another as you'd have
  Another deal with you:
What you're unwilling to receive,
  Be sure you never do.

YVONNE M. KHIN — Isaac Watts, *Divine and Moral Songs for Children,* c. 1717

Therefore all things whatsoever ye would that men should do to you, do ye even so to them: for this is the law and the prophets.

Matthew 7:12

What you do not want done to yourself, do not do to others.

Confucius
The Confucian Analects, c. 500 B.C.

No one of you is a believer until he desires for his brother that which he desires for himself.

Sunnah (Islam)

What is hateful to you do not do to your fellowman. That is the entire Law: all the rest is commentary.

The Talmud

Anything worth doing is worth doing well.

KAY BAILEY — My father

If a thing's worth doing, it's worth doing well.

KAREY BRESENHAN — Any number of old Texas grandmothers, including mine, Ella Glaeser Pearce

What is worth doing is worth doing well.

SEMBER HARTMAN — My grandmother

Whatever is worth doing at all, is worth doing well.

IONE McINTYRE — Philip Dormer Stanhope, Earl of Chesterfield
Letters,
March 10, 1746

Always finish what you start.

ANITA MURPHY — Old saying

Either do not attempt at all, or go through with it.

Ovid, 1st century B.C.

It is better never to have begun a good work, than having begun it, to stop.

Venerable Bede
Ecclesiastical History of the English People,
8th century

People will forget how fast you did the job, but they will remember how well you did it.

LAHOMA BUTLER RACKLEY

Stella Johnson Butler,
my mother

It only takes a little while to rip out those ugly stitches, and it will be forgotten. But if you leave them in, they will be seen forever.

MILLIE LEATHERS

First said to me when
I was three or four,
and repeated to every
basic quiltmaking class
I ever taught

Ease and speed in doing a thing do not give the work lasting solidity or exactness of beauty.

Plutarch
Life of Pericles,
1st century A.D.

Where there's a will there's a way.

SHEILA M. GROMAN

My husband's grandfather

Either I will find a way or I will make one.

Sir Philip Sidney, mid-16th century

The block of granite which was an obstacle in the pathway of the weak becomes a stepping-stone in the pathway of the strong.

Thomas Carlyle, 19th century

Heart to God, hands to man.

ANITA MURPHY

One of my students

Put your hands to work and your hearts to God.

Mother Ann Lee, c. 1774

If you want something done, do it yourself.

DOROTHY BETTIS — A saying I grew up with

If you would have a faithful servant, and one that you like, serve yourself.

Benjamin Franklin

If you want a job done, ask a busy person to do it.

SHARYN CRAIG — Saying

If you want a job well done, select a busy person—the other kind has no time.

Elbert Hubbard, c. 1900

Nothing ventured, nothing gained.

SHEILA M. GROMAN — My father-in-law

For he that naught n' assaieth, naught n' acheveth.

Geoffrey Chaucer
Troilus and Criseyde,
c. 1385

An ounce of prevention is worth a pound of cure.

SHEILA M. GROMAN — My dad

A stitch in time saves nine.

SHEILA M. GROMAN
SEMBER HARTMAN — My grandmother

Meet the disease at its first stage.

Persius
Satires, 1st century A.D.

Measure a thousand times and cut once.

Persian proverb

Waste not, want not.

SEMBER HARTMAN
PAULA LEDERKRAMER
JUDY REHMEL

My grandmother

And willful waste, depend upon it,
Brings, almost always, woeful want!

Ann Taylor
Hymns for Infant Minds, 1810

You get what you pay for.

SHEILA M. GROMAN

My dad, quoting exactly from Gabriel Biel, *Expositio Canonis Missae*, 15th century

Take what you want from life, and then pay for it.

Proverb

Beauty is as beauty does.

JOSEPH F. HOLLINGSHEAD — Old saying

In your clothes avoid too much gaudiness; do not value yourself upon an embroidered gown; and remember that a reasonable word, or an obliging look, will gain you more respect than all your fine trappings.

Sir George Savile
"Advice to a
Daughter," 1688

There is no beautifier of complexion, or form, or behavior, like the wish to scatter joy and not pain around us.

Ralph Waldo
Emerson, 1860

It is more blessed to give than to receive.

IONE McINTYRE — Acts 20:35

He that does good to another, does good also to himself, not only in the consequences, but in the very act; for the consciousness of well-doing is, in itself, ample reward.

Seneca, 1st century A.D.

. . . our life is what our thoughts make it.

DORIS L. SCOTT

Marcus Aurelius *Meditations*, 2nd century

To different minds, the same world is a hell, and a heaven.

Ralph Waldo Emerson, *Journal*, December 20, 1822

A friend in need is a friend indeed.

SHEILA M. GROMAN

My mom

Nothing is more friendly to a man than a friend in need.

Plautus
Epidicus, 2nd–3rd century B.C.

Love is friendship is love.

SHEILA M. GROMAN

My son Todd, age eight

Life is to be fortified by many friendships. To love and be loved is the greatest happiness of existence.

Sydney Smith, 18th–19th century

We would worry much less what other people think of us if we knew how infrequently they did it.

BETH GUTCHEON

My mother, quoting my grandmother

How much time he gains who does not look to see what his neighbor says or does or thinks, but only at what he does himself . . . .

Marcus Aurelius
Meditations,
2nd century

There's no kettle so crooked but what there's a lid to fit it.

JEAN RAY LAURY

My Dutch
grandmother

No man is born into the world whose work
Is not born with him . . . .

James Russell Lowell
"A Glance Behind the
Curtain," 1843

The weakest among us has a gift, however seemingly trivial, which is peculiar to him and which worthily used, will be a gift to his race . . . .

John Ruskin,
19th century

Often our worst fears are never realized.

MARIANNE FONS

Verlen Kruger,
my brother-in-law

Some of your hurts you have cured,
   And the sharpest you still have survived,
But what torments of grief you endured,
   From evils which never arrived.

Ralph Waldo
Emerson
"Borrowing," 1867

Don't tell me that worry doesn't do any good. I know better. The things I worry about don't happen.

Author unknown

There isn't a family in town that can hang a shingle on their door saying "No trouble here."

MARIANNE FONS

Our daughter's
teacher quoting a
community leader

Man that is born of a woman is of few days, and full of trouble.

Job 14:1

Sufficient unto the day is the evil thereof.

VIRGINIA AVERY

Matthew 6:34

We can easily manage, if we will only take, each day, the burden appointed for it. But the load will be too heavy for us if we carry yesterday's burden over again today, and then add the burden of the morrow to the weight before we are required to bear it.

John Newton,
18th century

Life is too short for strife.

ELLY SIENKIEWICZ

Donald Ross
Hamilton, my father

Life is too short to waste . . .
[In] quarrel or reprimand: . . . .

Ralph Waldo
Emerson, *Poems*
"To J.W.," 1847

This too shall pass.

SHARYN CRAIG
VIRGINIA AVERY
SALLY MEDVIDOVICH

My mother

It is said an Eastern monarch once charged his wise men to invent him a sentence to be ever in view, and which should be true and appropriate in all times and situations. They presented the words: "And this, too, shall pass away." . . . How chastening in the hour of pride! How consoling in the depths of affliction!

Abraham Lincoln
Address, Wisconsin
State Agricultural
Society, Milwaukee,
September 30, 1859

And as an interesting and thought-provoking postscript, we offer the following look at another point of view on this subject of folk wisdom.

Few maxims are true from every point of view.

Luc de Clapiers
Vauvenargues
Reflexions et Maximes, c. 1747

All maxims have their antagonistic maxims; proverbs should be sold in pairs . . . .

William Mathews
19th century

If you want a thing well done, do it yourself.

. . . there are lots of people who can do it just as well, leaving you the time to do something you really enjoy.

ELAINE SPARLIN

Anything worth doing is worth doing well.

Some things are best done quickly in order to get on to quilting time.

ELAINE SPARLIN

Cleanliness is, indeed, next to Godliness.

John Wesley
"Sermon 93,
On Dress,"
18th century

Reasonably clean is good enough.

ELAINE SPARLIN

Never put off until tomorrow what you can do today.

Nonsense! You might not have to do it at all tomorrow.

ELAINE SPARLIN

. . . time is money.

Benjamin Franklin
"Advice to a Young
Tradesman," 1748

. . . if you are quick you can steal money, or if you are robbed you can earn more, but when time is gone it's irreplaceably gone.

PENNY RIGDON

Live and let live.

Friedrich von Schiller
Wallenstein's Camp,
1798

Live and help live.

CARLA HASSEL

If at first you don't succeed, try, try again.

If "at second" you don't succeed, try a different way.

CARLA HASSEL

If at first you don't succeed, try again. Then quit. There's no use being a damn fool about it.

THERESA MILLETT W.C. Fields

The Hand of Friendship

Oh, the comfort—the inexpressible comfort
of feeling safe with a person.
Having neither to weigh thoughts,
    Nor measure words—but pouring them
All right out—just as they are—
Chaff and grain together—
Certain that a faithful hand will
Take and sift them—
Keep what is worth keeping—
and with a breath of kindness
Blow the rest away.

AMI SIMMS

Dinah Maria Mulock
Craik, "Friendship"

. . . the only way to have a friend is to be one.

MARGARET M. CAVIGGA
CARLA HASSELL

Ralph Waldo Emerson
"Friendship," 1841

Stay is a charming word in a friend's vocabulary.

JOANNE KOST

Amos Bronson Alcott

May the world
  hug you today
With its warmth and love
And whisper a joyful tune
  in your heart
And may the wind
  carry a voice
That tells you
  there is a friend
Sitting in another corner
  of the world
Right now
Wishing you well.

LaVONNE R. HANLON

Donna Abate
from a Blue Mountain
Arts card, 1984

The ornament of a house is the friends that frequent it.

JUDY ROBBINS

Ralph Waldo Emerson
"Domestic Life," 1860

Friendship's a word to few confined
The offspring of a noble mind
A generous warmth which fills the breast
And better felt than e'er expressed.

MARY GOLDEN

Author unknown
Embroidered on a
sampler, 1933

. . . old friends is always best, 'less you can catch a new one that's fit to make an old one out of . . . .

BLANCHE L. CONNOLLY

Sarah Orne Jewett
The Country of the Pointed Firs, 1896

The hand that gives gathers.

JOANNE KOST

John Ray
English Proverbs, 1670

True friends are like diamonds,
  Precious but rare;
False ones like autumn leaves,
  Found everywhere.

DOROTHY MEISEL

Author unknown
Written in an autograph book, 1893

Count your age by friends, not years
Count your life by smiles, not tears.

JOANNE KOST

Author unknown

. . . what did she do for clothin' when she needed to replenish, or rising for her bread, or the piecebag that no woman can live long without?

Sarah Orne Jewett
The Country of the Pointed Firs, 1896

I have long been haunted by this image of "Poor Joanna" who voluntarily exiled herself to a desolate island after being crossed in love. There she lived, died and was buried, never again setting foot on the mainland. A sad and baffling fate, especially for a woman "that loved her friends."

CARTER G. HOUCK

And you know I never lost anything by giving things away.

JOHN RICE IRWIN

Clemmie Pugh, age 100, Monterey, Tennessee, quoted in *A People and Their Quilts*, by John Rice Irwin, 1984

The friend who can be silent with us in a moment of despair or confusion, who can stay with us in an hour of grief, who can tolerate not knowing, not curing, not healing, and face with us the reality of our powerlessness, that is the friend who cares.

ELAINE MILES

Henri Nouwen

Heart's Desire

Ah Love! could you and I with Fate conspire
To grasp this sorry Scheme of Things entire,
  Would not we shatter it to bits—and then
Re-mould it nearer to the Heart's Desire!

SALLY MEDVIDOVICH

The Rubáiyát of Omar Khayyám XCIX,
11th–12th century
Translated by Edward Fitzgerald, 1859

I pray that risen from the dead
  I may in glory stand.
I need no crown upon my head,
  But a needle in my hand.

I've never learned to sing or play,
  So let no harp be mine;
From birth unto my dying day,
  Plain sewing's been my line.

Therefore, accustomed to the end
To plying useful stitches,
I'll be content if asked to mend
The little angels' breeches.

SHIRLEY CONLON
DOROTHY S. FINLEY

Eugene Field
"Grandma's Prayer," 1882

I must go down to the seas again, to the lonely sea and the sky,
And all I ask is a tall ship and a star to steer her by,
And the wheel's kick and the wind's song and the white sail's shaking,
And a gray mist on the sea's face, and a gray dawn breaking.

I must go down to the seas again, for the call of the running tide
Is a wild call and a clear call that may not be denied;
And all I ask is a windy day with the white clouds flying,
And the flung spray and the blown spume, and the sea gulls crying.

I must go down to the seas again, to the vagrant gypsy life,
To the gull's way and the whale's way where the wind's like a whetted knife;
And all I ask is a merry yarn from a laughing fellow-rover,
And quiet sleep and a sweet dream when the long trick's over.

SHIRLEY CONLON

John Masefield
"Sea Fever," 1902

When I am an old woman I shall wear purple
With a red hat which doesn't go, and doesn't suit me.
And I shall spend my pension on brandy and summer
  gloves
And satin sandals, and say we've no money for butter.
I shall sit down on the pavement when I'm tired
And gobble up samples in shops and press alarm bells
And run my stick along the public railings
And make up for the sobriety of my youth.
I shall go out in my slippers in the rain
And pick the flowers in other people's gardens
And learn to spit.

You can wear terrible shirts and grow more fat
And eat three pounds of sausages at a go
Or only bread and pickle for a week
And hoard pens and pencils and beermats and things
  in boxes.

But now we must have clothes to keep us dry
And pay our rent and not swear in the street
And set a good example for the children.
We must have friends to dinner and read the papers.

But maybe I ought to practise a little now?
So people who know me are not too shocked and
  surprised
When suddenly I am old, and start to wear purple.

Jenny Joseph
"Warning," 1974

BARBARA S. BOCKMAN
DORIS A. RABEY

I'd like to collect three things: time, space, and the money to enjoy them.

PENNY RIGDON

Margaret Todd, my friend and one of the founders of the National Quilting Association

If no one ever marries me—
  And I don't see why they should,
For nurse says I'm not pretty,
  And I'm seldom very good—

If no one ever marries me
  I shan't mind very much,
I shall buy a squirrel in a cage
  And a little rabbit-hutch;

I shall have a cottage near a wood,
  And a pony all my own,
And a little lamb, quite clean and tame,
  That I can take to town.

And when I'm getting really old—
  At twenty-eight or nine—
I shall buy a little orphan-girl
  And bring her up as mine.

EMILY J. WALDEN

Laurence Alma-Tadema
"If No One Ever Marries Me," 1897

Piece, piece, piece, and lo, a counterpane.
May each person resting here
Find peace, sweet peace
And ne'er encounter pain.

MARY GOLDEN

Author unknown
Recited by Lenice Bacon

But the conceited man did not hear him. Conceited people never hear anything but praise.

"Do you really admire me very much?" he demanded of the little prince.

"What does that mean—'admire'?"

"To admire means that you regard me as the handsomest, the best-dressed, the richest, and the most intelligent man on this planet."

"But you are the only man on your planet!"

"Do me this kindness. Admire me just the same."

HELEN KELLEY

Antoine de Saint-Exupéry, *The Little Prince*, 1943

We had a pet chameleon once who was in love with a wind-up clock. He just loved to hear it tick, and would strut around it for hours, inflating his throat sack, trying to get its attention. With all the quartz and electronic clocks today, I'm sure his love-life would have been much different.

BETTY TREASURE

Home Treasure

A man's best things are nearest him, lie close about his feet.

MARGARET M. CAVIGGA

Richard Monckton Milnes
"The Men of Old"

As he hurried along, eagerly anticipating the moment when he would be home again among the things he knew and liked, the Mole saw clearly that he was an animal of tilled field and hedgerow, linked to the ploughed furrow, the frequented pasture, the lane of evening lingerings, the cultivated garden-plot. For others the asperities, the stubborn endurance, or the clash of actual conflict, that went with Nature in the rough; he must be wise, must keep to the pleasant places in which his lines were laid and which held adventure enough, in their way, to last for a lifetime.

BLANCHE L. CONNOLLY

Kenneth Grahame
The Wind in the Willows, 1908

Who can find a virtuous woman? for her price is far above rubies.

The heart of her husband doth safely trust in her, so that he shall have no need of spoil.

She will do him good and not evil all the days of her life.

She seeketh wool, and flax, and worketh willingly with her hands . . . .

She layeth her hands to the spindle, and her hands hold the distaff.

She stretcheth out her hand to the poor; yea, she reacheth forth her hands to the needy . . . .

Strength and honour are her clothing; and she shall rejoice in time to come.

She openeth her mouth with wisdom; and in her tongue is the law of kindness.

She looketh well to the ways of her household, and eateth not the bread of idleness.

Her children arise up, and call her blessed; her husband also, and he praiseth her,

Many daughters have done virtuously, but thou excellest them all.

Favour is deceitful and beauty is vain: but a woman that feareth the Lord, she shall be praised.

Give her the fruit of her hands; and let her own works praise her in the gates.

Proverbs 31:10–13, 19–20, 25–31

I am a person who wants to be able to defend what it is I do, especially when, as in the case of my quilting and needlework, it affects the other members of my

family. Although neither my husband nor my children question the many hours I spend on my quilt-related activities, I feel the need to give reasons. The Bible, for me, is the most unimpeachable source of information, and it is there I go for excuses. The above seems to have been written not only for me, but for all quilters. What better justification could we have for our work?

SANDRA L. HATCH

Where we love is home, home that our feet may leave but not our hearts.

HAZEL CARTER

Oliver Wendell Holmes, "Homesick in Heaven," 1871

Blessed is the house where the experiences that count are not crowded out by those that don't.

KAREN BRAY

Author unknown

Homeward Bound

Life's a voyage that's homeward bound.

Herman Melville

What interests me is the waking in the morning, the progress from the familiar to the slightly odd, to the rather strange, to the totally foreign, and finally to the outlandish. The journey, not the arrival matters; the voyage, not the landing.

JOAN SCHULZE

Paul Theroux
The Old Patagonian Express, 1979

No two human beings have ever made, or will ever make, exactly the same journey in life.

THERESA MILLETT

Sir Arthur Keith

You shall take pleasure in the time while you are seeking, even though you obtain not immediately that which you seek; for the purpose of the journey is not only to arrive at the goal, but also to find enjoyment by the way.

RODERICK KIRACOFE

One of the "Four Rules for Contentment of Mind," author unknown, but given to me by my aunt, Helen Kiracofe Brubaker

"What is the Way?" a monk questioned his spiritual master. "The Way is your daily life," the master replied.

EMILY J. WALDEN

Author unknown

All travel is circular—the Grand Tour is just the inspired person's way of heading home.

JOAN SCHULZE

Paul Theroux

Honeybee

You will get more with honey than with vinegar.

ANITA MURPHY — Old saying

For he who'd make his fellow, fellow, fellow creatures wise,
Should always gild the philosophic pill.

BLANCHE L. CONNOLLY — William S. Gilbert
"I've Jibe and Joke,"
The Yeoman of the Guard, 1888

If your outgo exceeds your income then your upkeep will be your downfall.

JUDY REHMEL — Bill Earle

Don't push it, let it fall.

JEFFREY GUTCHEON — Duke Ellington

There's always room for improvement. It's the biggest room in the house.

SHEILA M. GROMAN — Author unknown

Behold the turtle. He makes progress only when he sticks his neck out.

SEMBER HARTMAN — James Bryant Conant

Angels can fly because they take themselves lightly.

CARLA HASSELL — Author unknown

Millions long for immortality who do not know what to do with themselves on a rainy Sunday afternoon.

ELAINE MILES — Susan Ertz

When you have lemons, make lemonade.

ANITA MURPHY — Author unknown

Give some people an inch and they think they're a ruler.

IONE McINTYRE — Author unknown

There is so much good in the worst of us, and so much bad in the best of us, that it hardly becomes the rest of us, to talk about ANY of us.

CARLA HASSELL — Author unknown

No matter what your lot in life, be sure to build something on it.

IONE McINTYRE — Author unknown

Training is everything. The peach was once a bitter almond; cauliflower is nothing but cabbage with a college education.

SEMBER HARTMAN — Mark Twain
Pudd'nhead Wilson, 1894

The ladder of life is full of splinters.

HAZEL CARTER — Author unknown

Nothing is impossible for the man who does not have to do it himself.

JUDY REHMEL — Author unknown

House on the Hill

I doubt that any house was really kept with perfect balance between order and personal accomplishments.

Ralph Waldo Emerson
The Journals and Notebooks

There was such a thing as women's work and it consisted chiefly . . . in being able to stand constant interruption and keep your temper.

SUELLEN MEYER

May Sarton
Mrs. Stevens Hears the Mermaids Singing, 1965

Woman's work is never done.

KAREY BRESENHAN

Proverb
(and eternal verity)

Blessed is she who has a room of her own
for she shall have peace and quiet.
She shall have a desk safe from sticky fingers
and file cabinets inviolate to an obsessive-compulsive
husband
with his own fail-safe, cross-reference system.
Blessed is she who has a place of her own
for she shall have colors that show the dirt,
sharp objects that need not be put away
and a chair for tossing clothes.
Blessed is she who has twelve feet by twelve feet
in her name
for she shall have a door that locks,
thick walls that mute the children's cries
and a refuge from mid-afternoon phone calls
from friends who know she is at home and cannot
be sincerely occupied.
Blessed is she who has a room of her own
And one hour a day to spend there.

ODETTE G. TEEL

Toby D. Schwartz
Mercy Lord, My Husband's in the Kitchen and Other Equal Opportunity Conversations with God, 1981

The very existence of messes is a debatable issue. Like beauty, they exist in the eye of the beholder.

JOYCE GROSS

Jean Ray Laury
The Creative Woman's Getting-It-All-Together-at-Home Handbook, 1977

At the worst, a house unkept cannot be so distressing as a life unlived.

THERESA MILLETT — Rose Macaulay

Milly Amos used to say that if a woman was to see all the dishes that she had to wash before she died, piled up before her in one pile, she'd lie down and die right then and there.

SYDNE YANKO-JONGBLOED — Eliza Calvert Hall
Aunt Jane of Kentucky, 1907

Relentless press of little things;
Eternal haste to do them all;
The prior claim upon our days
Relinquished to the trivial.

Our obligations never paid,
But endless and imperative.
O Life, why must you always leave
So little time to live?

BLANCHE L. CONNOLLY — Adelaide Love
"The Lien"

A creative woman may have cobwebs in her house, but not in her head.

KATHY MUNKELWITZ — Author unknown

A creative mess is better than tidy idleness.

BETTY TREASURE — Author unknown

Every woman needs a wife.

RUTH GREEN — Margaret Mead

Hyacinths

If of thy mortal goods thou art bereft,
And from thy slender store two loaves alone to thee
  are left
Sell one, and with the dole
Buy hyacinths to feed thy soul.

JANE BLAIR
HELEN YOUNG FROST

Muslih-uddin Saadi
Gulistan, 1258

I meant to do my work today—
  But a brown bird sang in the apple tree,
And a butterfly flitted across the field,
  And all the leaves were calling me.

And the wind went sighing over the land,
  Tossing the grasses to and fro,
And a rainbow held out its shining hand—
  So what could I do but laugh and go?

JOYCE AUFDERHEIDE

Richard Le Gallienne
"I Meant to Do My
Work Today," 1913

. . . Man [Woman] shall not live by bread alone . . . .

ELAINE SPARLIN

Matthew 4:4

The Mole had been working very hard all the morning, spring-cleaning his little home. First with brooms, then with dusters; then on ladders and steps and chairs, with a brush and a pail of whitewash; till he had dust in his throat and eyes, and splashes of whitewash all over his black fur, and an aching back and weary arms . . . . Spring was moving in the air above and in the earth below and around him, penetrating even his dark and lowly house with its spirit of divine discontent and longing. It was small wonder then, that he suddenly flung down his brush on the floor, said, "Bother!" and "O blow!" and also "Hang spring-cleaning!" and bolted out of the house without even waiting to put on his coat.

BLANCHE L. CONNOLLY

Kenneth Grahame
The Wind in the Willows, 1908

I have laid aside business, and gone a-fishing.

EMILY J. WALDEN

Isaak Walton
The Compleat Angler, 1653

Jagged Edge

It is a pity that doing one's best does not always answer.

Charlotte Bronte
Jane Eyre, 1847

Kindness is easily forgotten, since it never sticks or sinks so deeply as an insult.

LOUISE O. TOWNSEND

Calderón de la Barca
The Phantom Lady, 1629

. . . God's Plan is often a front for men's plans and a cover for inadequacy, ignorance and evil.

GENEVIEVE GURACAR

Mary Daly
Beyond God the Father, 1973

Once riding in old Baltimore,
  Heart-filled, head-filled with glee,
I saw a Baltimorean
  Keep looking straight at me.

Now I was eight and very small,
  And he was no whit bigger,
And so I smiled, but he poked out
  His tongue, and called me, "Nigger."

I saw the whole of Baltimore
  From May until December;
Of all the things that happened there
  That's all that I remember.

BLANCHE L. CONNOLLY

Countee Cullen
"Incident," 1925

The self-hatred that destroys is the waste of unfulfilled promise.

MARGARET J. MILLER

Author unknown

Why do you seek gold when our land has such lovely flowers?

ELAINE MILES

Last words of Peru's Inca ruler, Atahualpa, before being strangled by Francisco Pizarro's men.

Nobody has the right to throw you into a sea of empty responsibilities.

MARGARET J. MILLER

Moss Hart
from a clipping on the
bulletin board in
Nancy Crow's studio

Ah good taste! What a dreadful thing! Taste is the enemy of creativeness.

JOE CUNNINGHAM

Pablo Picasso

Joseph's Coat

Once there was a girl who needed a coat, but she had very little money so she worked very hard and bought some beautiful black material.

She made herself the wished-for coat. She wore it every day and it made her feel good, but then the coat wore out, which made her feel sad. But, as she was throwing the coat away, she thought, "There is still some good material left in the coat, I can make a jacket."

So she made a jacket, and wore it every day and it made her feel good, but one day the jacket wore out. She was very sad until she thought, "There is still some good material left in the jacket, I can make a vest."

She made herself a vest and she wore it every day and it made her feel good, but the vest wore out. She was going to throw it out, but wait—

"I can make a hat." So she made a hat and wore it every day. It made her feel very good until it seemed there was no more use left, but no, maybe she could cover a button.

So she did just that and wore it every day and it made her feel so good until finally she saw she would have to throw her button away, but wait—

There was just one more thing she could do and that was to tell this story.

HELEN BITAR A folk tale

The first lady I interviewed was a 98-year-old quilter. She had started making a quilt for each child, niece, and nephew 35 years ago, but before she finished the next generation was arriving, and then the third. She said she had 8 more quilts to make for that third generation and the first great-great granddaughter had arrived three months before. Her comment was, "You know, I just don't think I'm going to have time to die."

DOLORES A. HINSON

I had a pattern for a quilt which I called "The Day We Dropped the Atom Bomb on Japan." It described how I experienced World War II. It has a picture of my dad, brother, and our best friends, Big Jack and Little Jack, fishing on Grand River Lake in Oklahoma. Mom and Aunt Beth are on the shore.

I had driven all around Southwest Missouri looking for a quilter willing to do this pattern. I found her living with her husband in a very small trailer almost on top of a mountain. Her husband, a construction worker, was away, so I began by introducing myself, telling her what I was about, and, as I could see she was interested, I got my pattern from the car, all the materials I had purchased for the work and spread them out to show her how it would go.

I never really noticed that the pattern almost completely covered the trailer's interior. I was so happy to have found someone to do my design, I didn't consider how this project might affect my quilter's life when her husband came home.

Two weeks later this postcard arrived from my quilter:

Dear Mr. Larson,

Come quick and get the Hell out of here.

Sincerely . . ."

EDWARD LARSON

In 1977, approaching a divorce, I was filled with fear and tension. Would I be able to carry on, supporting myself and living decently, or would I become a "bag lady"? One day, in search of the answers, I drove to an isolated lake and sat staring at the water. I wanted to have my entire future planned out instantly so I would not have to worry any more.

As I was sitting there, a young fisherman went by and called out, "All I want is one fish." *He passed by, sure that he would get something. He was not thinking of every meal he would have to provide for the rest of his life, he was only concerned with having a fish for that night.*

From then on I started facing one day at a time, enjoying each, and accepting what I could accomplish within it, instead of being anxious about all the tomorrows.

CHARLOTTE PATERA

When I was a child, I spent many happy weeks during the summer at my grandparent's farm in Alabama. This was a real working farm, and all the adults kept busy from early dawn until bedtime. My grandmother, Mary Elizabeth McNaron Hughes, had unbelievable responsibilities compared to most of us today. Besides being a quilt-maker (to keep warm), she canned and preserved everything they ate in the winter. When a given crop was ready, it had to be taken care of that day.

One day I was enjoying my childly leisure, swinging lazily on the big front porch. Grandmama called to me, "Doris, what are you doing?"

"I'm resting." (From what I'm not sure.)

"Well," said Grandmama, "while you're resting, shell the peas."

DORIS HOOVER

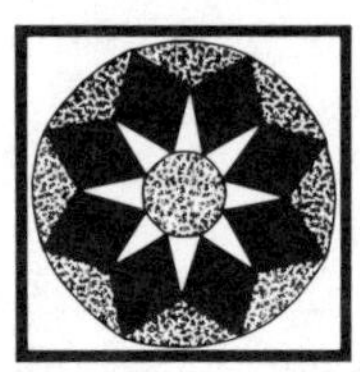

Kansas Sunflower

Whereas, Kansas has a native wild flower common throughout her borders, hardy and conspicuous, of definite, unvarying and striking shape, easily sketched, moulded, and carved, having armorial capacities, ideally adapted for artistic reproduction, with its strong, distinct disk and its golden circle of clear glowing rays—a flower that a child can draw on a slate, a woman can work in silk, or a man can carve on stone or fashion in clay; and

Whereas, this flower has to all Kansans a historic symbolism which speaks of frontier days, winding trails, pathless prairies, and is full of the life and glory of the past, the pride of the present and richly emblematic of the majesty of a golden future, and is a flower which has given Kansas the world-wide name, "the sunflower state"; therefore,

Be it enacted by the Legislature of the State of Kansas:

That the helianthus or wild native sunflower is hereby made, designated and declared to be the state flower and floral emblem of the state of Kansas.

JEAN MITCHELL

Statute enacted in 1903 making the sunflower the official state flower of Kansas

King's Crown

The high prize of life, the crowning fortune of a man, is to be born with a bias to some pursuit, which finds him in employment and happiness.

Ralph Waldo Emerson
The Conduct of Life,
1860

And whatsoever ye do, do it heartily, as to the Lord . . .

KAY BAILEY — Colossians 3:23

Do all your work as though you had a thousand years to live, and as you would if you knew you must die tomorrow.

BARBARA S. BOCKMAN
JEAN MITCHELL — Mother Ann Lee, c. 1774

Get happiness out of your work or you may never know what happiness is.

EMILY J. WALDEN

Elbert Hubbard

In the glad morning of blooming youth
These various threads I drew,
And now behold this finished piece
Lies glorious to the view.
So when bright youth shall charm no more
And age shall chill my blood,
May I review my life and say,
"Behold—my works are good."

YVONNE M. KHIN

Author unknown
Embroidered on a sampler, 1831

Work is love made visible.

LINDA PLATT

Kahlil Gibran
The Prophet, 1923

Wherefore I perceive that there is nothing better, than that a man should rejoice in his own works; for that is his portion: for who shall bring him to see what shall be after him?

JEAN MITCHELL

Ecclesiastes 3:22

You can't eat for eight hours a day nor drink for eight hours a day nor make love for eight hours a day . . . the only thing you can do for eight hours a day, day after day, is work.

JOAN SCHULZE

William Faulkner, 1958

Laziness has killed more people than hard work.

JOHN RICE IRWIN

Lucy Stooksbury, Anderson County, Tennessee, quoted in *A People and Their Quilts* by John Rice Irwin, 1984

God give me work for the rest of my life, and life for the rest of my work.

ELAINE MILES

Hindu proverb

Do your best to present yourself to God as one approved, a workman who has no need to be ashamed, rightly handling the word of truth.

MILDRED LOCKE

II Timothy 2:15 Revised Standard Version

We see human thought and feeling best and clearest by seeing it through something solid that our hands have made.

SUELLEN MEYER

Eudora Welty

Every man's task is his life-preserver.

THERESA MILLETT

Ralph Waldo Emerson
The Conduct of Life,
1860

Blessed are they who have found their work; let them ask no other blessedness. They have a work, a life purpose . . . .

BLANCHE L. CONNOLLY

Thomas Carlyle
Past and Present,
1843

Nonesuch

Whoever thinks a faultless piece to see
Thinks what ne'er was, nor is, nor e'er shall be.

PATRICIA J. MORRIS

Alexander Pope
An Essay on Criticism, 1711

Only God is perfect.

NAN TOURNIER

Author unknown

The only people who never make mistakes are those who never do anything.

JUDY REHMEL

Lloyd Morris
This Week Magazine, 1966

You have only failed when you have failed to try.

MARY SCHAFER

Author unknown

If you're not failing at something, you're not doing anything.

JOAN SCHULZE — Woody Allen

Success is going from failure to failure without loss of enthusiasm.

THERESA MILLETT — Winston Churchill

Success is failure turned inside out.

LOIS K. IDE — Author unknown

The only way to avoid mistakes is to gain experience. The only way to gain experience is to make mistakes.

MARY SCHAFER — Author unknown

Nothing would be done at all if man waited 'til he could do it so well no one could find fault with it.

SEMBER HARTMAN
VIVIAN RITTER
LOUISE O. TOWNSEND — John Henry Cardinal Newman

The difference between success and failure is decided by little things when you are least aware of it.

IONE McINTYRE — Martin Vanbee

All of us are constantly called upon to make important decisions and it's irrational to expect to be correct all the time. It's terribly important not to be torn by our mistakes.

ELAINE MILES — Dr. Owens

Even God cannot change the past.

EMILY J. WALDEN — Agathon, c. 415 B.C.

Maturity lies in accepting reality, not in demanding perfection.

JUDY ROBBINS — Author unknown

Nonsense

A little nonsense now and then
Is relished by the wisest men.

Nursery rhyme

It is important to do one crazy thing every day, just to keep sane.

JEAN RAY LAURY — Author unknown

You first parents of the human race . . . who ruined yourself for an apple, what might you not have done for a truffled turkey?

ELAINE MILES — Anthelme Brillat-Savarin

No man is lonely while eating spaghetti—it requires too much attention.

ELLY SIENKIEWICZ — Christopher Morley

Keep this kitchen clean. Eat out.

JUDY FLORENCE — Author unknown

One evil action every day
Will keep psychiatrists away.
Relax, and once a day at least,
Contrive to be a perfect beast.
Free, uninhibited, untamed.
Unscrupulous and unashamed.
In short, a normal man or woman,
Instead of something superhuman!

SALLY MEDVIDOVICH — Ralph Humphries

If we all got our just desserts, none of us would be eating ice cream.

SHIRLEY CONLON — Jo Coudert
Advice from a Failure, 1965

The ant has made himself illustrious
By constant industry industrious.
What! . . . would you be calm and placid,
If you were full of formic acid?

HELEN KELLEY — Ogden Nash
"The Ant,"
Verses from 1929 On,
1935

Yu see quilts wer wun ove her speshul gifts: she run strong on the bed-kiver question. Irish chain, star ove' Texas, sun-flower, nine dimunt, saw teeth, checker board an' shell quilts: blue, an' white, an' yaller an' black coverlids, and callicker-cumfurts reigned triumphan' about her hous'. They wer packed in drawers, laying in shelfs full, wer hung dubbil on lines in the lof, packed in chists, piled on cheers, an wer everywhar, even ontu the beds, an' wer changed every bed-makin. She told everybody she cud git tu listen tu hit that she ment to give every durn one ove them tu Sal when she got married. Oh, lordy! what es fat a gal es Sal Yardley cud ever du wif half ove em, an' sleeping wif a husband at that, is more nor I ever cud see through. Jis' think ove her onder twenty layer ove quilts in July, an' yu in thar too.

DOROTHY COZART

George Washington Harris, "Mrs. Yardley's Quilting," c. 1850

Lying in bed would be an altogether perfect and supreme experience if only one had a coloured pencil long enough to draw on the ceiling.

BLANCHE L. CONNOLLY

G.K. Chesterton
Tremendous Trifles, 1909

Spring has sprung, the grass is ris,
I wonder where the flowers is?

SHEILA M. GROMAN

Author unknown

If it's true that we are what we eat, how come we all aren't light, new and improved?

LOIS K. IDE — Ivern Ball

When in trouble or in doubt,
Run in circles, scream and shout.

JAN HALGRIMSON — Author unknown (These words are to be used when all appears lost. It helps even more if said in a funny voice.)

A voice came to me saying: "Cheer up, things could be worse." So I cheered up, and, sure enough, things got worse.

IONE McINTYRE — Author unknown

Optical Illusion

'Twixt the optimist and the pessimist
The difference is droll:
The optimist sees the donut
But the pessimist sees the hole.

McLandburgh Wilson,
c. 1915

Nothing ain't so bad but that it couldn't be worse.

ELLY SIENKIEWICZ

Aunt Orpha Hamilton,
Mole Hill, West
Virginia, mid-20th
century

He drew a circle that shut me out—
Heretic, rebel, thing to flout.
But Love and I had the wit to win:
We drew a circle that took him in!

JEAN DUBOIS

Edwin Markham
"Outwitted," 1915

You don't trust to luck for the caliker to put your quilt together with; you go to the store and pick it out for yourself, any color you like. There's folks that can never see anything but the dark side, and always looking for trouble, and treasurin' it up after they git it, and they're puttin' their lives together with black, jest like you would put a quilt together with some dark, ugly color. You can spoil the prettiest quilt pieces that ever was made jest by puttin' 'em together with the wrong color, and the best sort o' life is miserable if you don't look at things right and think about 'em right.

HELEN M. ERICSON

Eliza Calvert Hall
Aunt Jane of Kentucky, 1907

"No sight so sad as that of a naughty child," he began, "especially a naughty little girl. Do you know where the wicked go after death?"

"They go to hell," was my ready and orthodox answer.

"And what is hell? Can you tell me that?"

"A pit full of fire."

"And should you like to fall into that pit, and be burning there for ever?"

"No, sir."

"What must you do to avoid it?"

I deliberated a moment; my answer, when it did come, was objectionable: "I must keep in good health, and not die."

THERESA MILLETT

Charlotte Bronte
Jane Eyre, 1847

Well, at least there's no angry mob outside.

Hannah Fons, 1987

This was an 11-year-old's response to her Papa one night at the supper table when, in a complaining mood, he was listing, not only what was wrong in the world, but what was not working in our house.

MARIANNE FONS

A father gives his pessimist son a room full of wonderful toys for Christmas. The son is indifferent and thinks there must be a catch. To his optimist son he gives a pile of manure. The son starts to dig through it and tells his father, "There must be a pony!"

CHARLOTTE PATERA

From the television film, *There Must Be a Pony*, 1986

Path Through the Woods

The woods are lovely, dark and deep,
But I have promises to keep,
And miles to go before I sleep,
And miles to go before I sleep.

JOYCE AUFDERHEIDE
HELEN KELLEY

Robert Frost
"Stopping by Woods on a Snowy Evening," 1923

In the midst of winter, I finally learned there was in me an invincible summer.

LOUISE O. TOWNSEND

Albert Camus
The Fall, 1956

To live in the presence of great truths and eternal laws — that is what keeps a man patient when the world ignores him, and calm and unspoiled when the world praises him.

EMILY J. WALDEN

Honoré de Balzac

Catch the sunshine, don't be grieving
O'er that darksome billow there.
Life's a sea of stormy billows,
We must meet them everywhere.
Pass right through them, do not tarry,
Overcome the heaving tide,
There's a sparkling gleam of sunshine
Waiting on the other side.

YVONNE M. KHIN

Isaac Watts
Divine and Moral Songs for Children, c. 1715

God hath not promised
  Skies always blue,
Flower-strewn pathways
  All our lives through;
God hath not promised
  Sun without rain,
Joy without sorrow,
  Peace without pain.

But God hath promised
  Strength for the day,
Rest for the laborer,
  Light on the way;
Grace for the trial,
  Help from above,
Unfailing sympathy,
  Undying love.

CUESTA BENBERRY
IONE McINTYRE

Author unknown
Hearth and Home Magazine, July 1929

I am, being human, born alone.
I am, being woman, hard beset.
I live by squeezing from a stone
The little sustenance I get.

BETS RAMSEY

Eleanor Wylie
"Let No Charitable Hope," 1923

You may not live a hundred years, but you may encounter a hundred problems.

U KHIN

A Burmese proverb

In every mortal's span of years
There will be seasons
When the soul is lean and bare . . .
When foundations crumble
And the heart lies down
To wait for strength's renewal
Like a fallow field . . .

THERESA MILLETT

Clara S. Hoff
"Fallow Field," c. 1940

Whatever doesn't kill you will make you stronger.

KATY CHRISTOPHERSON
SEMBER HARTMAN

Friedrich Nietzsche
The Twilight of the Idols, 1888

It takes both the sun and the rain to make a beautiful rainbow.

MARY SCHAFER
LOUISE O. TOWNSEND

Author unknown

For me who goes,
for you who stays—
two autumns.

MARINA SALUME

Buson, "Parting"

Water, when it must, plunges downward. It flows over rocks without breaking and fills all the low places and nothing can make it lose its magic.

BETH GUTCHEON

From *The I Ching*, or
Book of Changes,
12th century B.C.

Patience Corners

Patience and the mulberry leaf become a silk robe.

LOUISE O. TOWNSEND — Chinese proverb

If you add only a little to a little and do this often, soon that little will become great.

CINDY V. DAVIS — Hesiod
Works and Days,
8th century B.C.

Poco à poco . . . ("Little by little . . .")

RUTH GREEN — Spanish phrase

They also serve who only stand and wait.

JEAN EITEL — John Milton
"On His Blindness,"
1652

If you have the patience to hand-quilt, then you shall have the patience to handle whatever life brings to you.

MARY LOUISE KITSEN — Lillie Shepherd Wright, my great-grandmother

If you are patient in one moment of anger, you will escape a hundred days of sorrow.

KAREN BRAY — Chinese proverb

Be patient with yourself. Grow in your own way in your own time.

MARY SCHAFER — Author unknown

Always remember, when we are green we are growing.

ANITA MURPHY — Sister Philomina, my teacher when I was seven

Patience and persistence are the keywords to success.

IONE McINTYRE — Author unknown

'Tain't worthwhile to wear a day all out before it comes.

BLANCHE L. CONNOLLY — Sarah Orne Jewett, *The Country of the Pointed Firs*, 1896

I'll think of it all tomorrow . . . after all, tomorrow is another day.

HELEN R. SCOTT — Margaret Mitchell, *Gone with the Wind*, 1936

One day at a time.

RODERICK KIRACOFE — Slogan from Al-Anon

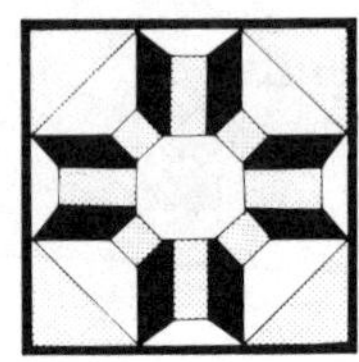

Prosperity

Prosperity is more than an economic condition; it is a state of mind.

Frederick Lewis Allen

Not Land, but Learning
Makes a man Complete.
Not Birth, but Breeding
Makes him truly Great.
Not Wealth but Wisdom
Does adorn his State.
Virtue, not Honour
Makes him Fortunate.
Learning, Breeding, Wisdom;
Get these three
Then Wealth and Honour
Will attend on thee.

YVONNE M. KHIN

Author unknown
Embroidered on a sampler, 1910

. . . success should be measured by whether you can get up in the morning and feel good about what you're doing with your life.

LOUISE O. TOWNSEND — David French, c. 1983

To live content with
    small means; to seek
elegance rather than
    luxury, and refinement
rather than fashion;
. . . .
        to study hard,
        think quietly,
        talk gently,
        act frankly;
to listen to stars and birds,
    to babes and sages with open heart;
      to bear all cheerfully,
        do all bravely, await occasions, never hurry.
          In a word, to let the spiritual, unbidden and
          unconscious
            grow up through the common.

DIXIE HAYWOOD — William Henry Channing, "My Symphony"

It is a great blunder in the pursuit of happiness not to know when we have got it; that is, not to be content with a reasonable and possible measure of it.

ELAINE MILES — Dr. Samuel Johnson

There is nothing I can give you
which you have not,
But there is much, very much that
while I cannot give it, you can take.

No heaven can come to us unless our hearts
find rest in today. Take heaven!
No peace lies in the future which is not hidden
in this present instant. Take peace!

The gloom of the world is but a shadow.
Behind it, yet within reach, is joy.
There is a radiance and a glory in the darkness, could
we but see,
and to see we have only to look. I beseech you to look.

Life is so generous a giver, but we, judging its gifts by
their covering, cast them away as ugly, or heavy or
hard.
Remove the covering, and you will find beneath it
a living splendor, woven of love, by wisdom, with
power.

Welcome it, grasp it, and you touch the angel's hand
that
brings it to you. Everything we call a trial, a sorrow,
or
a duty, believe me, that angel's hand is there; the gift
is there,
and the wonder of an overshadowing presence.
Our joys too: be not content with them as joys.
They, too, conceal diviner gifts.

And so, at this time, I greet you.
Not quite as the world sends greeting, but with
profound esteem and with the prayer that for you now
and
forever, the day breaks, and the shadows flee away.

DOROTHY MEISEL — Fra Giovanni, 1513

The purpose of life is not to be happy. The purpose of life is to matter, to be productive, to have it make some difference that you live at all. Happiness, in the ancient, noble sense, means self-fulfillment and is given to those who use to the fullest whatever talents God or luck or fate bestowed upon them.

JANET B. ELWIN — Leo Rosten
Captain Newman M.D., 1962

Human felicity is produced not so much by great pieces of good fortune that seldom happen, as by little advantages that occur every day.

BLANCHE L. CONNOLLY — Benjamin Franklin
Autobiography, 1771

Not what we have, but what we use,
Not what we see, but what we choose—
These are the things that mar or bless
The sum of human happiness.

IONE McINTYRE — C. Urmy

Providence

Commit thy way unto the Lord; trust also in him; and he shall bring it to pass.

VIRGINIA AVERY — Psalms 37:5

The will of God will never lead you where the grace of God cannot keep you.

JOANNE KOST — Proverb

Trust in the Lord with all thine heart; and lean not unto thine own understanding.

In all thy ways acknowledge him and he shall direct thy paths.

MARY EMMA ALLEN — Proverbs 3:56

Let go and let God.

RODERICK KIRACOFE — Slogan from Al-Anon

Therefore I say unto you, Take no thought for your life, what ye shall eat, or what ye shall drink; nor yet for your body, what ye shall put on. Is not the life more than meat, and the body than raiment?

Behold the fowls of the air: for they sow not, neither do they reap, nor gather into barns; yet your heavenly Father feedeth them. Are ye not much better than they?

Which of you by taking thought can add one cubit unto his stature?

And why take ye thought for raiment? Consider the lilies of the field, how they grow; they toil not, neither do they spin:

And yet I say unto you, That even Solomon in all his glory was not arrayed like one of these.

Wherefore, if God so clothe the grass of the field, which today is, and tomorrow is cast into the oven, shall he not much more clothe you, O ye of little faith . . .

Take therefore no thought for the morrow: for the morrow shall take thought for the things of itself. Sufficient unto the day is the evil thereof.

JUDY S. TOMLONSON — Matthew 6:25-30, 34

But they that wait upon the Lord shall renew their strength; they shall mount up with wings as eagles; they shall run, and not be weary; and they shall walk and not faint.

MARY EMMA ALLEN — Isaiah 40:31

I will lift up mine eyes unto the hills, from whence cometh my help.

HELEN KELLEY
ELLY SIENKIEWICZ

Psalms 121:1

God may not always meet your schedule, but he will always be on time.

JUDY S. TOMLONSON

Alex Haley

. . . seek ye first the kingdom of God, and his righteousness; and all these things shall be added unto you.

DONNA D. GAROFALO

Matthew 6:33

And we know that all things work together for good to them that love God, to them who are the called according to his purpose.

MARY EMMA ALLEN
JEAN DUBOIS

Romans 8:28

This is the day which the Lord hath made; we will rejoice and be glad in it.

BONNIE LEONARD
MILDRED LOCKE

Psalms 118:24

Man proposes, but God disposes.

Thomas à Kempis
The Imitation of Christ, c. 1427

When I started flying back in 1948 . . . DC–3, *21 passengers, few of today's instruments and technical advancements . . . weather was a big item. One of the pilots used to say this to allay the fears of the understandably leery passengers.*

ANITA MURPHY

Whither shall I go from thy spirit? or whither shall I flee from thy presence?

If I ascend up into heaven, thou art there: if I make my bed in hell, behold, thou art there.

If I take the wings of the morning, and dwell in the uttermost parts of the sea;

Even there shall thy hand lead me, and thy right hand shall hold me.

MARY EMMA ALLEN
JUDY S. TOMLONSON

Psalms 139:7-10

Be gentle to the less fortunate who passeth by,
Except for God's mercy there passeth thy.

JOSEPH F. HOLLINGSHEAD

Folk rhyme

The Lord is my shepherd; I shall not want.

He maketh me to lie down in green pastures: he leadeth me beside the still waters.

He restoreth my soul: he leadeth me in the paths of righteousness for his name's sake.

Yea, though I walk through the valley of the shadow of death, I will fear no evil: for thou art with me; thy rod and thy staff they comfort me.

Thou preparest a table before me in the presence of mine enemies: thou anointest my head with oil; my cup runneth over.

Surely goodness and mercy shall follow me all the days of my life: and I will dwell in the house of the Lord for ever.

BETH GUTCHEON Psalms 23

Puss-in-the-Corner

The cat purrs to please himself alone.

GWEN MARSTON — Chinese proverb

I don't know the key to success, but the key to failure is trying to please everybody.

LOUISE O. TOWNSEND — Bill Cosby

Self-trust is the first secret of success.

MARGARET M. CAVIGGA — Ralph Waldo Emerson

It is important to have confidence in your own ideas. Once you are happy with your own work you can appreciate rather than envy that of others.

FRAN SOIKA

Under all circumstances we must never desert ourselves.

EMILY J. WALDEN

Louisa Adams, wife of John Quincy Adams, sixth president of the United States

I yam what I yam and that's all what I yam.

Popeye

By acknowledging the things about yourself that you cannot change and by changing what you can, all without worrying about what other people think, you will be happy with the unique combination that constitutes you and only you.

ART SALEMME

This above all: to thine own self be true,
And it must follow, as the night the day,
Thou canst not be false to any man.

HELEN KELLEY
MILDRED L. MORGON

William Shakespeare
Hamlet, 1600

Always remember that you are unique, just like everyone else.

MARY SCHAFER

Author unknown

The light you seek is in your own lantern.

KATHY MUNKELWITZ — Old saying

All the wonders you seek are within yourself.

MARY SCHAFER — Author unknown

Know thyself.

Inscription at the
Delphic Oracle
c. 650 B.C.

So that you are better able to "be yourself."

PENNY RIGDON

If you really put a small value upon yourself, rest assured that the world will not raise the price.

ELAINE MILES — Author unknown

I am what I am.
I do what I do.
And if you do not like it,
Then, to hell, my love, with you!

KAREY BRESENHAN — Author unknown

When I was quite young, a relative asked me, "Are you your mama's girl or your daddy's girl?"

I looked at my father and he said, "You tell them you are yourself's girl."

JEAN MITCHELL

Blunder ahead with your own personal view.

BARBARA L. CRANE

Robert Henri
The Art Spirit, 1923

After a while you learn
The subtle difference between
holding a hand
and chaining a soul
and you learn
that love doesn't mean
leaning
and company doesn't always mean
security.
And you begin to learn
That kisses aren't contracts and
presents aren't promises
and you begin to
accept your defeats
with your head up and your eyes ahead
with the grace of a woman
not the grief of a child
and you learn
To build all your roads on today
because tomorrow's ground is

too uncertain for plans
and futures have a way of falling down
in mid-flight.
After a while you learn
That even sunshine burns
if you ask too much
So you plant your own garden
and decorate your own soul
instead of waiting for someone to bring you flowers
and you learn
that you really can endure
that you really are strong
and you really do have worth
And you learn
And you learn
with every goodbye
You learn . . .

DOROTHY MEISEL

Veronica Shoffstall
"After a While," 1971

No one can make you feel inferior without your consent.

SHEILA M. GROMAN
LOUISE O. TOWNSEND

Eleanor Roosevelt

Argue for your limitations, and sure enough, they're yours.

SUSAN K. TURBAK

Richard Bach
Illusions, 1977

At 50 I decided to do more of what I wanted to do, stopped doing many things I didn't want to do, and gave up worrying about those things I had no control over.

FRAN SOIKA

You can't live by "standards." Each life is unique. Life is given to you to be yourself as thoroughly and entirely as you can. But it's hard work.

JOAN SCHULZE

Jeanne Moreau
"W" *Magazine*,
October 1985

. . . you can't please anyone until you can please yourself.

LOUISE O. TOWNSEND

Candice Bergen
from an interview,
January 1, 1985

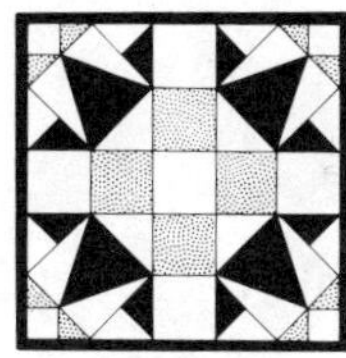

Quilter's Delight

I'd druther quilt than eat on the hungriest day that ever I seen.

JOHN RICE IRWIN

Ethel Hall, Viper, Kentucky, quoted in *A People and Their Quilts* by John Rice Irwin, 1984

Do you own a handmade quilt? Count yourself fortunate if you do. Doubly so if your quilt was made especially for you, because it says in its own quiet way "someone loves you"—a message no factory-made blanket with its dual controls and its expensive price tag can quite convey. Perhaps it is this one message alone that has helped quilting survive the machine age as no other home art has done.

JOHN MANGIAPANE

Progressive Farmer, July 1973
(I tuck the above into every quilt that I sell or give away.)

Quilters have a life's work instead of a job. We carry our life's focus wherever we go.

FLAVIN GLOVER

Jean Ray Laury

The best place to learn about quilts is quilts.

PENNY RIGDON

Doris Bowman,
Curator of Textiles
Smithsonian
Institution

Spring's a soft coverlet,
  Dainty and light;

Summer's a patchwork quilt,
  Colors all bright;

Autumn's a counterpane,
  Flamboyant sight;

Winter's a baby's quilt,
  Fluffy and white.

ERNEST B. HAIGHT

Isabelle Hooper
Haight from *Practical Machine-Quilting for the Homemaker* by
Ernest B. Haight,
1974

The joy of each day is directly proportionate to the hours spent in quilting.

VIVIAN RITTER

Helen Kelley
"Loose Threads,"
Quilter's Newsletter Magazine, May 1983

Enjoy cozy winter naps,
Discard not those fabric scraps.

JOSEPH F. HOLLINGSHEAD

Folk rhyme

My grandmother, Bessie Wright Lyman, who was the town dressmaker, lived with us when I was a girl in Plainville, Connecticut. One spring, the owner of Cook's Tavern, a fine restaurant, brought grandmother two bolts of flowered calico to make colonial dresses for his waitresses. When the man told Granny she could keep all the unused material she replied, "Thank you for presenting me with next winter's quilts."

MARY LOUISE KITSEN

A needle in the hand is worth two in another place.

MARY M. CONROY

Author unknown

If there are not a few sprinkles of blood from pricked fingers on a finished quilt—the quilter just wasn't trying.

DOLORES A. HINSON

Retha Gambaro, my quilt teacher

The next time the world seems cold to you, try kindling a fire of love to warm it. A good way to start might be to make a quilt for someone.

VIVIAN RITTER

Theo Eson
"Grandma's Corner,"
Quilter's Newsletter Magazine, May 1978

Quilting is not a matter of life and death: it is more important than that.

AMI SIMMS

Author unknown

Oh Lord! I love it! I can set all day long and quilt. I love to set and quilt when it's snowing outside—just set there and quilt and watch the snow comin' down.

JOHN RICE IRWIN

Flossie Cornett, Jeff, Kentucky, quoted in *A People and Their Quilts* by John Rice Irwin, 1984

"There ain't nothin' like a piece o' caliker for bringin' back old times, child . . . this quilt," she said, "I made out o' the pieces o' my children's clothes, their little dresses and waists and aprons. Some of 'em's dead, and some of 'em's grown and married . . . but when I set down and look at this quilt and think over the pieces, it seems like they all come back, and I can see 'em playin' around the floors and goin' in and out, and hear 'em cryin' and laughin' and callin' me . . . ."

Eliza Calvert Hall
Aunt Jane of Kentucky, 1907

My first quilt effort was a Grandmother's Flower Garden done over papers, English method. I used scraps from years of making clothes for my daughter and as I went along, I too could happily recall when each dress was made and for what occasion. I have since given that first quilt to my daughter and while not very expertly done, nor finely quilted, we both love it. She remembers hating to try everything on; I *remember a child in a pretty new dress.*

DORIS A. RABEY

Quilters don't make quilts to get rich.

EDWARD LARSON

Eventually I came to feel something more . . . about quiltmaking than that it was a good way for me to pass the time. I came to feel that American quilts are not just a series of artifacts but an important part of the history of American women. Their beauty, their ingenuity, and also the vast amount of repetition, the great number of cautious variations on familiar themes, in some important way constitutes a record of what life has been like for American women. Not the least important is the fact that while the quilts contain a great deal of testimony, almost all of it is mute. American women have long had hearts and minds, but only a very few have had voices.

JUDY FLORENCE

Beth Gutcheon
The Quilt Design Workbook, 1976

It's all I have to bring today—
This, and my heart beside—

JANE BLAIR

Emily Dickinson,
c. 1858

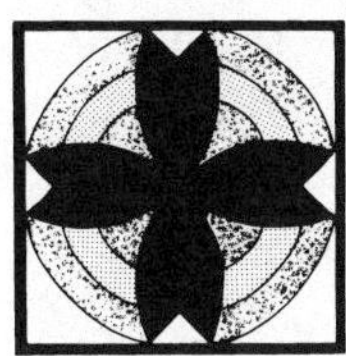

Rainbow

Imagination is the rainbow bridge between spirit and matter.

NANCY HALPERN — Owen Barfield

. . . that rapturous meeting between the artist's private vision and the shimmering world of objects.

THERESA MILLETT — Nancy Hale, *The Life in the Studio*, 1969

You can't get all the way just on facts. To get to a wonderful place you have to let your imagination take you the last leg.

RHODA R. COHEN — Garrison Keillor "Prairie Home Companion," 1986

It is through art and art only that we can realize our perfection, through art and art only that we can shield ourselves from the sordid perch of actual existence.

MARGARET M. CAVIGGA — Oscar Wilde

Things as they are,
Are changed on my blue guitar.

DIANA LEONE — Author unknown

It's Poetry that's taken by surprise
In the most rigid of geometries.

JOAN SCHULZE — May Sarton
"Italian Garden,"
Selected Poems of May Sarton, 1978

We have made a space to house our spirit, to give form to our dreams . . . .

GENEVIEVE P. GURACAR — Judy Chicago
"Let Sisterhood be Powerful," 1973

Art is the appearance of effortlessness and the perfectly right choice. What is hidden are the sloppy paint cans, the crumpled pages on the floor, the cancelled ideas and impulses.

JOAN SCHULZE — Author unknown

[Artists'] essential effort is to catapult themselves wholly, without holding back one bit, into a course of action without having any idea where they will end up. They are like riders who gallop into the night, eagerly leaning on their horse's neck, peering into a blinding rain. And they have to do it over and over again. When they find that they have ridden and ridden—maybe for years, full-tilt—in what is for them a mistaken direction, they must unearth within themselves some readiness to turn direction and to gallop off again. They may spend a little time scraping off the mud, resting the horse, having a hot bath, laughing and sitting in candlelight with friends. But in the back of their minds they never forget that the dark driving run is theirs to make again. They need their balances in order to support their risks. The more they develop an understanding of all their experience—the more it is at their command—the more they carry with them into the whistling wind.

MARION L. HUYCK

Ann Truitt
Daybook: The Journal of an Artist, 1982

What was any art but an effort to make a sheath, a mould in which to imprison for a moment the shining elusive element which is life itself — life hurrying past us and running away, too strong to stop, too sweet to lose?

ELAINE MILES

Willa Cather
The Song of the Lark, 1915

Life without industry is guilt; industry without art is brutality.

GEORGIA J. BONESTEEL

John Ruskin
Lectures on Art, 1870

. . . 'tis God-like to create.

John Godfrey Saxe
"The Library"

In the very ancient account in Genesis the first comment is "God created." Later it says that "God created mankind in his own image and likeness," suggesting that man, in this sense, is like God the Creator. Of all life on earth only mankind creates, invents, visualizes, imagines that which is not.

SARAH HASS

A pattern is the picture of the essence of an object, an object's very life; its beauty is of that life. In fact, it would be truer to say that its beauty is that life staring the pattern maker in the face. A pattern may lie on a table inert, just ink on paper, but it is the child of vision . . . . A good pattern is pregnant with beauty. The maker of a pattern draws the essence of the thing seen with his own heartbeat, life to life.

NANCY HALPERN

Sōetsu Yanagi
The Unknown Craftsman, 1972

There's so much more to basket making than just learning how to do it. You have to feel it in your heart, and you have to cherish the gift of being a basket maker.

MARGARET J. MILLER

Lena Bommelyn
quoted in "Northwest California Basketry,"
by Pam Mendelsohn
Southwest Art,
June 1983

Art is the making of a thing that has to be.

BETS RAMSEY

St. Thomas Aquinas

Spider Web

Humankind has not woven the web of life. We are but one thread within it. Whatever we do to the web, we do to ourselves. All things are bound together. All things connect. Whatever befalls the earth befalls also the children of the earth.

Chief Seattle, 1854

To the man who is truly ethical all life is sacred, including that which from the human point of view seems lower in the scale.

WILLOW ANN SOLTOW

Albert Schweitzer

A man is a thousand parts. All of them other people. Those he loved, those he did not, those who merely passed through his life. And the total of him is the sum of all of them added together, divided by each other, subtracted from each other and multiplied individually and cumulatively. I looked around the room. And there I was.

ELLY DYSON

Harold Robbins
The Inheritors, 1971

The world is our home. It is also the home of many, many other children, some of whom live in faraway lands. They are our world brothers and sisters.

NORMA BRADLEY ALLEN

F.B. Carpenter
Around the World with Children

The basis of any tolerable society—from the small society of the family up to the great society of the State—depends upon its members learning to love. By that I do not mean sentimentality or possessive emotion. I mean the steady recognition of others' uniqueness and a sustained intention to seek their good. In this, freedom and charity go hand in hand and they both have to be learned. Where better than in the home? and by whom better taught than the parents, especially the mother?

GEORGIA J. BONESTEEL

Adlai E. Stevenson

You can no longer save your family, your tribe or nation. You can only save the whole world.

EMILY J. WALDEN

Margaret Mead

If I am not for myself, who is for me?
But if I am only for myself, what am I?

PAULA NADELSTERN

Pirke Avod, "The Sayings of Our Fathers," *The Talmud* 1:14

We are all pearls, and the string is God.

BETH GUTCHEON — Muktananda, a Hindu teacher

Children trained to extend justice, kindness and mercy to animals become more just, kind and considerate in their relations with each other . . . . The cultivation of the spirit of kindness to animals is but the starting point toward that larger humanity which includes one's fellow of every race and clime. A generation of people trained in these principles will solve their international difficulties as neighbors and not as enemies.

WILLOW ANN SOLTOW — Statement issued by the National PTA Congress of 1933

He prayeth best, who loveth best
All things both great and small;
For the dear God who loveth us,
He made and loveth all.

JEAN EITEL — Samuel Taylor Coleridge, *The Ancient Mariner*, 1798

We need another and wiser and perhaps a more mystical concept of animals . . . . We patronize them for their incompleteness, for their tragic fate of having taken form so far below ourselves. And therein we err, and greatly err. For the animal shall not be measured by man. In a world older and more complete than ours they move finished and complete, gifted with extensions of the senses we have lost or never attained, living by voices we shall never hear. They are not brethren, they are not underlings; they are other nations, caught with ourselves in the net of life and time, fellow prisoners of the splendor and travail of the earth.

WILLOW ANN SOLTOW

Henry Beston
The Outermost House,
1928

Steps to Glory

The longest journey starts with a single step.

IONE McINTYRE — Chinese proverb

Just keep working.

JAN HALGRIMSON — Folk wisdom

Life must be lived as play, playing certain games, making sacrifices, singing and dancing, and then a man will be able to propitiate the gods, and defend himself against his enemies, and win the contest.

GWEN MARSTON — Plato

So become a list maker. Most successful people are compulsive about written lists.

PATRICIA J. MORRIS — Michael Korda

I shall study and get ready, and perhaps one day my chance will come.

KATY CHRISTOPHERSON — Abraham Lincoln

Genius is 1% inspiration and 99% perspiration.

NELL COGSWELL — Thomas A. Edison
Life, 1932

Once, in China, a man gave an artist money
to make a painting of a fish.
The man waited several years,
and whenever he saw the artist,
he asked for the painting.
After several more years, the man grew angry.
He went to the artist's house
and demanded the painting.
The artist took a piece of paper,
dipped his brush in paint,
and with ease dashed off
the most beautiful painting of a fish.
The man was astonished.
"If it was so simple," he said,
"why didn't you do it sooner?"
In reply the artist slid open a door.
Thousands of paintings of fish fell out.

NANCY HALPERN — Remy Charlip
JUDY ROBBINS — *Arm in Arm*, 1969

Diligence is the mother of good fortune.

EMILY J. WALDEN

Miguel de Cervantes
Don Quixote, 1605

When I was young I little thought
That wit must be so dearly bought,
But now experience tells me how
If I must thrive, then I must bow
And bend unto another will,
That I might learn both art and skill.

YVONNE M. KHIN

From a sampler

To do a common thing uncommonly well brings success.

MARSHA McCLOSKEY

Corita Kent

Sunbeam

Brighten the corner where you are.

RUTH GREEN — Protestant hymn

During a lifetime, an individual should devote all efforts to create happiness and enjoy it, and also keep it in store in society so that individuals of the future may also enjoy it.

BEE NEELEY KUCKELMAN — Ch'en Tu-shiu, *The New Youth,* Feb. 1918

Most folks are just about as happy as they make up their minds to be.

ELAINE SPARLIN — Abraham Lincoln

Bloom where you are planted.

NAN TOURNIER
LOUISE O. TOWNSEND — Author unknown

Laugh, and the world laughs with you;
Weep and you weep alone;
For the sad old earth must borrow its mirth,
But has trouble enough of its own.

MARGARET M. CAVIGGA

Ella Wheeler Wilcox
"Solitude," c. 1890

Experience is not what happens to you; it is what you do with what happens to you.

IONE McINTYRE

Aldous Huxley

We cannot control the events of our life, but we can control our reactions to these events.

LOIS K. IDE

Jo Petty

If you want to be happy—be.

LOUISE O. TOWNSEND

Liz Carpenter

I guess being kind is the most important thing in the world and you can't even see it.

HELEN M. ERICSON

Jean Bell Mosley
"Portrait for Molly"

Something had to be did, so I done it.

Popeye

In any life, crisis situations are bound to arise. When they do, don't just stand there indecisively, waiting for someone to take action. Instead, go into action yourself and know that Popeye would approve.

ART SALEMME

Do all the good you can,
In all the ways you can,
To all the souls you can,
In all the places you can,
At all the times you can,
With all the zeal you can,
As long as ever you can.

John Wesley
"Rule," c. late 18th century. Found in a 1934 collection of quotations among my aunt's belongings.

CARLA HASSEL

Do the best that you can in the time that you have.

Author unknown

IONE McINTYRE

Do the best you can in the place you are . . . and be kind.

JUDY ROBBINS

Scott Nearing

Do the best you can with what you have where you are.

Attributed to Martha Washington

Martha's descendant Catherine Murat must have found this motto useful on the Florida frontier in the mid-19th century as her husband, the interesting but eccentric Achille Murat, nephew of Napoleon Bonaparte, tried repeatedly—and vainly—to recoup the family fortune.

LACY BULLARD

It is not as important *who* you are and *where* you live as *what* you are and *how* you live.

MILDRED L. MORGON

Author unknown

Never fail to give or to be of use to others, for that giving is the source of true happiness.

CYRIL I. NELSON

Elinor Irwin Chase Holden, my grandmother

Despise evil and ungodliness, but not men of ungodliness or evil. These, understand . . . . In the time of your life, live—so in that wondrous time you shall not add to the misery and sorrow of the world . . . .

KATY CHRISTOPHERSON

William Saroyan
The Time of Your Life,
1939

Even the smallest good deed done is better by far than the grandest intention.

IONE McINTYRE

Treasured Verses,
1956

Life is short and we have not too much time for gladdening the hearts of those who are travelling the dark way with us. Oh, be swift to love! Make haste to be kind!

ELAINE MILES

Henri Frédéric Amiel

The way to create happiness: keep your heart free from hate, your mind from worry. Live simply, expect little, give much.

LOIS K. IDE

Norman Vincent Peale

The greatest thing you'll ever learn,
is just to love
and be loved in return.

JEFFREY GUTCHEON

Eden Ahbez
"Nature Boy," 1946

The fragrance always stays in the hand that gives the rose.

LOUISE O. TOWNSEND

Hada Bejar

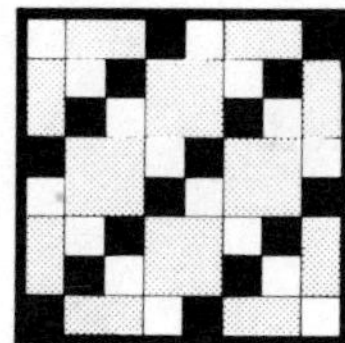

Three Steps

There are three natural classes of people: those who see, those who see when they are shown, and those who do not see.

Leonardo da Vinci,
c. 1500

Small minds discuss people,
Average minds discuss events,
Great minds discuss ideas.

SHEILA M. GROMAN

Author unknown

A man who works with his hands is a laborer; one who works with his hands and his brain is a craftsman; but one who works with his hands and his brains and his heart is an artist.

JINNY BEYER
MARY M. CONROY
JUDY FLORENCE

Louis Nizer

The grand essentials to happiness in this life are something to do, something to love, and something to hope for.

EMILY J. WALDEN — Joseph Addison

Have more than thou showest,
Speak less than thou knowest,
Lend less than thou owest.

BARBARA S. BOCKMAN — William Shakespeare
King Lear, 1606

The best doctors in the world are Doctor Diet, Doctor Quiet and Dr. Merryman.

BLANCHE L. CONNOLLY — Jonathan Swift
Polite Conversation, 1738

Youth is a gift of Nature,
Middle Age is a work of Art,
Old Age ain't for sissies.

ODETTE G. TEEL — Author unknown

My secret to living long and looking young: eat only one meal a day, wash your face with only cold water, and don't fall in love to the extent that you're a fool.

ELAINE MILES — Alberta Hunter, age 84

Wisdom is knowing what to do,
Knowledge is knowing how to do it,
Success is doing it.

SHEILA M. GROMAN

Author unknown

His words are fair, but his deeds are bad and his intentions much worse.

BLANCHE L. CONNOLLY

Chapuys, Spanish ambassador to the court of Henry VIII, speaking of Thomas Cromwell. (Cromwell was one of the king's foremost agents in dissolving, suppressing and confiscating the properties of the monasteries, and bringing about an absolute monarchy.)

I had three chairs in my house: one for solitude, two for friendship, three for society.

THERESA MILLETT

Henry David Thoreau
Walden, 1854

Time and Tide

Time and tide wait for no man.

English proverb

Dare to be wise—begin. He who postpones the hour of living is like the rustic who waits for the river to run out before he crosses.

CAROL P. CRABB

Horace
Epistles, 13 B.C.

Procrastination is the thief of time.

MARGARET M. CAVIGGA

Edward Young
Night Thoughts, 1742–1745

Don't make the mistake of letting yesterday use up too much of today.

IONE McINTYRE

Author unknown

The Moving Finger writes; and having writ,
Moves on: nor all your Piety nor Wit
  Shall lure it back to cancel half a Line,
Nor all your Tears wash out a Word of it.

JOYCE AUFDERHEIDE

The Rubàiyàt of Omar Khayyám LXXI, 11th–12th century
Translated by Edward Fitzgerald, 1859

Don't wait for the last judgment. It takes place every day.

LOUISE O. TOWNSEND

Albert Camus
The Fall, 1956

Don't put off until tomorrow what you can do today.

VIRGINIA AVERY
IRENE GOODRICH

Old saying

The way to get something done is to begin.

KAREN BRAY

Author unknown

Create, artist! Do not talk!

SARAH HASS

Johann Wolfgang von Goethe

Many fine things can be done in a day—if you don't make that day tomorrow.

IONE McINTYRE *Treasured Verses*

Rejoice at your life, for the time is more advanced than you would think.

ELAINE MILES Proverb

Ah, make the most of what we yet may spend,
Before we too into the Dust descend;
  Dust unto Dust, and under Dust, to lie,
Sans Wine, sans Song, sans Singer, and—sans End!

SALLY MEDVIDOVICH *The Rubáiyát of Omar Khayyám XXIV*, 11th–12th century Translated by Edward Fitzgerald, 1859

The Wonder of the World,
The Beauty and Power,
The Shapes of things,
Their Colors, Lights and Shades—
These, I saw.
Look ye also, while Life lasts.

THERESA MILLETT From a tombstone, Cumberland, England

Get at it.

JOYCE SCHLOTZHAUER

My mother

Tomorrow is the day on which lazy people work and fools reform.

CAROL P. CRABB

The Prairie Farmer
1860

In creating, the only hard part is to begin.

ROBERTA HORTON

Author unknown. "A heavy-duty thought" that appeared in the *San Francisco Chronicle* years ago.

Do not act as if you had ten thousand years to throw away. Be good for something while you live and it is in your power.

EMILY J. WALDEN

Marcus Aurelius
Meditations,
2nd century

In masks outrageous and austere
The years go by in single file;
But none has merited my fear,
And none quite escaped my smile.

SHIRLEY CONLON

Elinor Wylie
"Let No Charitable
Hope," 1923

Four ducks on a pond,
A grass-bank beyond,
A blue sky of spring,
White clouds on the wing:
What a little thing
To remember for years—
To remember with tears!

VIRGINIA AVERY

William Allingham

Time, you old gypsy man,
  Will you not stay,
Put up your caravan
  Just for one day?

BLANCHE L. CONNOLLY

Ralph Hodgson
"Time, You Old Gypsy
Man," 1913

Tree Everlasting

As my family planted for me so do I plant for my children.

SHEILA M. GROMAN — *The Talmud*

This I learned from the shadow of the tree,
That to and fro did sway against a wall,
Our shadow selves, our influence may fall
Where we ourselves can never be.

FLAVIN GLOVER — Anna Hamilton, "Influence," c. 1870

There are only two lasting bequests we can give our children. One is roots, the other wings.

DORIS HOOVER — Quoted by Hodding Carter in *Where Main Street Meets the River*, 1953

Write your name in kindness, love and mercy, on the hearts of thousands you come in contact with year by year; you will never be forgotten. No, your name, the deeds will be as legible on the hearts you leave behind as the stars on the brow of the evening. Good deeds will shine as the stars of heaven.

CARLA HASSEL

Patrick Reginald Chalmers

Since it is not granted us to live long, let us transmit to posterity some memorial that we at least lived.

THERESA MILLETT

Pliny the Younger, c. 100 A.D.

I like to make things out of wood
The older I get, the stronger I build
Am I trying to build immortality?
I don't think so
I know that whether I live or die
The things I make have a life of their own
Separate and apart
I just want them to have a good life
And long.
Like I've had
Thanks, God, for building me strong.

MARGARET J. MILLER

Elise Maclay
Green Winter—Celebrations of Old Age, 1977

Every experience deeply felt in life needs to be passed along — whether it be through words and music, chiseled in stone, painted with a brush, or sewn with a needle, it is a way of reaching for immortality.

LOUISE O. TOWNSEND

Thomas Jefferson

I've been a hard worker all my life, but 'most all my work has been the kind that "perishes with the usin'," . . . but when one o' my grandchildren sees one o' these quilts, they'll think about Aunt Jane, and, wherever I am then, I'll know I ain't forgotten.

I reckon everybody wants to leave somethin' behind that'll last after they're dead and gone. It don't look like it's worthwhile to live unless you can do that.

SUELLEN MEYER
DORIS A. RABEY
SYDNE YANKO-JONGBLOED

Eliza Calvert Hall,
Aunt Jane of Kentucky, 1907

A teacher affects eternity; he can never tell where his influence stops.

BLANCHE L. CONNOLLY

Henry Brooks Adams
The Education of Henry Adams, 1907

Making a quilt is like planting a tree.
It is an act of love and faith in the future.

MARGARET M. CAVIGGA
BETTINA HAVIG

Author unknown

I would like to believe when I die that I have given myself away like a tree that sows seeds every spring and never counts the loss, because it is not loss, it is adding to future life. It is the tree's way of being. Strongly rooted perhaps, but spilling out its treasure on the wind.

RHODA R. COHEN

May Sarton
Recovering, 1980

Wheel of Fortune

I'm Nobody! Who are you?
Are you—Nobody—Too?
Then there's a pair of us?
Don't tell! They'd advertise—you know!

How dreary—to be—Somebody!
How public—like a Frog—
To tell one's name—the livelong June—
To an admiring Bog!

JANE BLAIR — Emily Dickinson, c. 1861

Pleasing an audience means catering to its lowest common denominator; it is a kind of implied insult masquerading as a caress.

CARON L. MOSEY — Sydney J. Harris

No amount of planning will ever replace dumb luck.

JEAN V. JOHNSON — Author unknown

When one strives to reach the top, the one at the top must necessarily fall.

U KHIN — A Burmese proverb

Boasting of one's greatness to excess,
Will turn away those one hopes to impress.

JOSEPH F. HOLLINGSHEAD — Folk rhyme

Fortune is like glass—the brighter the glitter, the more easily broken.

BLANCHE L. CONNOLLY — Publilius Syrus, *Maxims*, c. 1st century B.C.

Wheel of Mystery

The fairest thing we can experience is the mysterious.

BARBARA L. CRANE — Albert Einstein

The world is still a miracle, wonderful, inscrutable, magical and more, to whosoever will think it.

SHEILA M. GROMAN — Thomas Carlyle

I seek
in moss and water,
plants, stones, drifting sand
and in the play of light and shadows,
Those deep forests, distant mountains
and vast mysterious beckoning places
almost remembered.

SUSAN K. TURBAK — Author unknown

The very commonplaces of life are components of its eternal mystery.

EMILY J. WALDEN — Gertrude Atherton

Be patient toward all that is unsolved in your heart . . . try to love the questions themselves like locked rooms and like books written in a very foreign tongue. Do not now seek the answers, which cannot be given to you because you would not be able to live them. And the point is, to live everything. Live the questions now. Perhaps you will then gradually, without noticing it, live along some distant day into the answer.

MARION L. HUYCK — Rainer Maria Rilke, *Letters to a Young Poet*, 1934

The man who cannot wonder . . . is but a Pair of Spectacles behind which there is no Eye.

THERESA MILLETT — Thomas Carlyle

A force is only visible in its effect, and it is the split second in which this effect becomes just barely visible that haunts me. The turns of life are secret.

BARBARA L. CRANE — Ann Truitt, *Daybook: The Journal of an Artist*, 1982

Wheel of Time

Preserve the old but know the new.

Chinese proverb

If men could learn from history, what lessons it might teach us! But passion and party blind our eyes, and the light which experience gives us is a lantern on the stern, which shines only on the waves behind us.

PATRICIA J. MORRIS

Samuel Taylor Coleridge, "On T. Allsop's Recollections"

Never forget the past, but never allow the past to dominate our future.

SHEILA M. GROMAN

David Ben-Gurion

If we open a quarrel between the past and the present, we shall find that we have lost the future.

LOUISE O. TOWNSEND

Winston Churchill

The only way tradition can be carried on is to keep inventing new things.

MICHAEL JAMES

Robert Davidson,
Haida Indian carver,
quoted in *Indian Artists at Work* by
Ulli Steltzer, 1976

There is no ending that is not a beginning.

SHEILA M. GROMAN

Henrietta Szold

What you have inherited from your fathers, earn over again for yourselves, or it will not be yours.

BLANCHE L. CONNOLLY

Johann Wolfgang von Goethe

. . . the historical sense involves perception, not only of the pastness of the past, but of its presence . . . .

MARY JO DALRYMPLE

T.S. Eliot
"Tradition and the Individual Talent,"
1920

Windflower

All the flowers of the spring
Meet to perfume our burying;
These have but their growing prime,
And man doth flourish but his time: . . .
Vain ambition of kings
Who seek by trophies and dead things
To leave a living name behind,
And weave but nets to catch the wind.

John Webster
"The Devil's Law
Case," 1623

Oh threats of Hell and Hopes of Paradise!
One thing at least is certain—*This* Life flies;
  One thing is certain and the rest is Lies;
The Flower that once has blown for ever dies.

SALLY MEDVIDOVICH

The Rubáyát of Omar Khayyám, LXIII,
11th–12th century
Translated by
Edward Fitzgerald,
1859

I met a traveller from an antique land
Who said: Two vast and trunkless legs of stone
Stand in the desert. Near them on the sand
Half sunk, a shattered visage lies, whose frown
And wrinkled lip and sneer of cold command
Tell that its sculptor well those passions read
which yet survive, stamp'd on these lifeless things,
the hand that mock'd them and the heart that fed;
And on the pedestal these words appear:
"My name is Ozymandias, king of kings:
Look on my works, ye Mighty, and despair!"
Nothing beside remains. Round the decay
of that colossal wreck, boundless and bare,
The lone and level sands stretch far away.

HELEN KELLEY

Percy Bysshe Shelley
"Ozymandias of
Egypt," 1817

The mighty are brought low by many a thing
Too small to name. Beneath the daisy's disk
Lies hid the pebble for the fatal sling.

EMILY J. WALDEN

Helen Hunt Jackson

All passes. Art alone
  Enduring stays to us;
The Bust outlasts the throne,—
  The Coin, Tiberius.

THERESA MILLETT

Théophile Gautier
"Ars Victrix," 19th
century

Oh ye that put your trust and confidence
In worldly joy and frail prosperity . . .
Remember death and look here upon me . . .
Your queen but late, and lo now here I lie . . .

If worship might have kept me, I had not gone.
If wit might have me saved, I needed not fear.
If money might have helped, I lacked none.
But O good God what availeth all this gear?
When death is come, thy mighty messenger,
Obey we must, there is no remedy;
Me hath he summoned, and lo now here I lie.

BLANCHE L. CONNOLLY

Sir Thomas More
"A Rueful Lamentation on the Death of Queen Elizabeth," written for the wife of Henry VII, 1503

Fear no more the heat o' the sun,
Nor the furious winter's rages;
Thou thy worldly task has done,
Home art gone, and ta'en thy wages;
Golden lads and girls all must,
As chimney-sweepers, come to dust.

ELAINE MILES

William Shakespeare
Cymbeline, 1609

World Without End

To every thing there is a season, and a time to every purpose under the heaven: . . . .

JEAN MITCHELL — Ecclesiastes 3:1

You could not step twice into the same river, for other waters are ever flowing onto you.

BEE NEELEY KUCKELMAN — Heraclitus

I looked again at the heap of quilts. An hour ago they had been patchwork and nothing more. But now! The old woman's words had wrought a transformation in the homely mass of calico and silk and worsted. Patchwork? Ah, no! It was memory, imagination, history, biography, joy, sorrow, philosophy, religion, romance, realism, life, love, and death: and over all, like a halo, the love of the artist for his work and the soul's longing for earthly immortality.

HELEN M. ERICSON — Eliza Calvert Hall, *Aunt Jane of Kentucky*, 1907

Morning has broken like the first morning,
  Blackbird has spoken like the first bird.
Praise for the singing
Praise for the morning
  Praise for the springing first from the Word.

Sweet the rain's new fall, sunlit from Heaven.
  Like the first dew fall on the first grass.
Praise for the sweetness of the wet garden
  Spring in the completeness where His feet pass.

Mine is the sunlight! Mine is the morning.
  Born of the one light Eden saw play!
Praise with elation
Praise every morning
  God's creation of the new day.

HELEN R. SCOTT

Eleanor Farjeon
"Morning Has
Broken," 1957
*Hymnbook of The
United Presbyterian
Church of U.S.A.*

I never behold the stars that I do not feel that I am looking in the face of God. I can see how it might be possible for a man to look down upon the earth and be an atheist, but I cannot conceive how he could look up into the heavens and say there is no God.

MILLY SPLITSTONE

Abraham Lincoln

It's linkage I'm talking about,
                                        and harmonies and structures
And all the various things that lock our wrists to the
  past.

Something infinite behind everything appears,
                                        and then disappears.

It's all a matter of how
                                        you narrow the surfaces.
It's all a matter of how you fit in the sky.

SUSAN K. TURBAK

Charles Wright
"The Other Side of the
River," *The New
Yorker*, April 5, 1982

And so the morning's gone. Was this to waste it
In a long foolish flowery meditation?
Time slides away, and how are we to taste it?
Within the floating world all is sensation.
And yet I see eternity's long wink
In these elusive games . . . .

JOAN SCHULZE

May Sarton
"A Flower-Arranging
Summer," *Selected
Poems of May Sarton*,
1978

The Contributors

Mary Emma Allen of Plymouth, New Hampshire, was born October 27, 1938, in Poughkeepsie, New York. Mary, who had a home-based quilting and patchwork business for several years, makes quilts on commission, is an editor for a corporate newsletter, a beauty/color consultant, and a newspaper and magazine columnist. Her "The Business of Patchwork," written under the byline of Mea Allen, has been a regular feature of *Quilt World Omnibook* since 1981. Mary's work has also appeared often in other publications such as *Quilt*.

"Quiltmaking," she says, "is one of those arts which forms a common bond among quiltmakers around the world and, once in the blood, is an activity the quilter can never give up."

Norma Bradley Allen, a native Texan, born in Plainview, and living in Cedar Hill, is a lecturer, film actress, and writer. Her work includes *The Quilters: Women and Domestic Art* (co-author), articles for numerous magazines and periodicals, a column for *The Dallas Times Herald*, and the series, "Quilters: Tales and Traditions," featured in *Quilter's Newsletter Magazine*.

"When I first 'paid attention' to the quilts and quilters of my heritage," Norma says, "I feared that I was in love with a dying art as well as a dying breed of artist. What a joy to watch the phoenix rise before there were too many ashes."

Joyce Aufderheide, born June 30, 1920, in Lake Wilson, Minnesota, has lived for 50 years in New Ulm, Minnesota, where, for some of those years, she had the Hands All Around Quilt Museum. A quilter, historian, and lecturer, Joyce possesses what she calls "an almost perfect quilt collection," parts of which have appeared in *Lady's Circle Patchwork Quilts*, *Quilter's Newsletter Magazine*, and *All Flags Flying*, by Robert Bishop and Carter Houck.

In 1977, one of the quilts from Joyce's collection, "Madelia Medallion," made by Marie Pedelty, was chosen to hang in the office of Vice President Walter Mondale as an example of American folk art. Of this occasion, she says, "I was asked to personally deliver the quilt to Mr. Mondale at the White House, and I don't believe I could ever top the thrill this gave me."

Virginia Avery was born and raised in Indiana, graduated from DePauw University, and arrived in New York by way of Detroit. She teaches, lectures, judges, designs, and writes, as well as makes original quilts and clothing. Her work has appeared frequently in such publications as *Lady's Circle Patchwork Quilts* and *Quilter's Newsletter Magazine*, and she is the co-author of *Encyclopedia of Needlework* and author of *The Big Book of Appliqué* and *Quilts to Wear*.

For rest and recreation, Virginia plays piano in a Dixieland jazz band called The King Street Stompers, and feels that "jazz and quilting are sisters under the skin, for you are always improvising on a theme." Of her life in quilting, she says, "I'm not dreaming the impossible dream — I'm living it."

Kathrine Elizabeth Leyerly Bailey, a native Minnesotan, was born April 16, 1922, in Sauk Rapids, and lives in Maple Plain. She was a member of the Women's Army Corps in World War II, had a tax and accounting business, and is the author of *The Sampler Quilt*, *To Make a Quilt*, *Quilting Stitchery: Books I, II, and III*, and *Quilt Your Christmas*, all published under her own imprint of Homeart. Kay contributes regularly to such magazines as *Quilt*, and writes fiction.

Her most important quilt-related accomplishment, she feels, has been promoting the idea, in both her writing and teaching, that quilting is "to be enjoyed by doing, using, or just looking."

Cuesta Benberry, born in Cincinnati, Ohio, has spent most of her life in St. Louis, Missouri, where she retired from the public schools as a reading specialist. She is also a certificated librarian. Cuesta, who has been collecting, cataloguing, documenting, and researching quilts and quilt patterns since the early 1960s, was history and research editor for *Nimble Needle Treasures* (published from 1969 to 1976), and writes frequently for *Quilters' Journal* and *Quilter's Newsletter Magazine*.

On November 8, 1983, Cuesta Benberry, selected "for her tireless contributions to two important aspects of quilting: history research and pattern collecting," was inducted into The Quilters' Hall of Fame. "I am gratified," she says, "that serious quilt research and quilt history are finally being recognized as a serious and legitimate discipline."

Dorothy Nola Bartle Bettis lives in Eugene, Oregon, where she was born March 29, 1906. Dorothy, who takes pleasure in helping and encouraging other quilters, has been an accomplished needlewoman from childhood, and a serious quilter since 1964. Her work has won many awards and been featured in *Lady's Circle Patchwork Quilts*, *Quilt Art '86 Engagement Calendar*, and *Quilters' Journal*.

The "making of quilts in their entirety" is Dorothy's great interest, but she also likes to have her talents challenged, and says, "When I chose to do a clamshell quilt, it was to find out why quilt literature said it was hard to do."

Jinny Beyer of Great Falls, Virginia, was born July 27, 1941, in Denver, Colorado, and lived for several years in India, Nepal, and Malaysia. A quiltmaker, teacher, lecturer, designer, and writer, who was inducted into The Quilters' Hall of Fame on September 29, 1984, Jinny's work has appeared in numerous publications including *Lady's Circle Patchwork Quilts*, *Quilter's Newsletter Magazine*, and *Quilters' Journal*. Among her achievements are the quilt "Ray of Light," first prize-winner in the 1978 *Good Housekeeping* Quilt Contest; the books *Patchwork Patterns*, *The Quilter's Album of Blocks and Borders*, *Medallion Quilts*, *A Six-Minute Mile*, and *The Scraplook;* and the videos *Palettes for Patchwork* and *Mastering Patchwork*.

Jinny feels her most important contributions to the world of quilting have been the books she's written and the fabrics she's designed because "they touch so many quilters across the country." Of quilting, she says, "[It] is a distinctly personal art form that can be perpetuated not only through the creation of new designs, but also in the interpretation and execution of the old."

Helen Bitar, born December 24, 1940, in Centralia, Washington, graduated from the University of Washington with a degree in printmaking, and lives in Portland, Oregon. She is a designer, artist, and craftsman whose quilt, "The Mountain from My Window," was one of the highlights of The New American Quilt Show (1976). This work, along with two others, is featured in *The Contemporary Quilt* by Patti Chase. Helen shares her creativity with the larger world through the medium of her front yard and the brightly painted objects and creatures that fill it.

As for swiftly passing time and all that yet remains to be done, her philosophy is to ". . . watch where I am in life and see if I am accomplishing what I want to do so when I reach the age of death I will not regret things I said I was going to do."

Jane Blair, who lives in Conshohocken, Pennsylvania, was born in nearby Philadelphia, May 8, 1926. A graduate of West Chester State University, she began seriously quilting in 1973. Since then, her quilts have appeared on book and magazine covers, the walls of museums, corporations, and private collections, and in numerous publications including *American Quilter* and *Quilter's Newsletter Magazine*. Jane does a limited amount of teaching and lecturing, but feels her real work is the making of quilts.

Of this she says, "[It] begins with quilt blocks created and named by quilters from the past . . . . I am interested in innovative design and color, but still want the end result to be more pleasing to the eye than shocking to the soul — somewhere between the faded gems of the past and the vivid harshness of the present. If my work looks traditional to some and contemporary to others, I have achieved the blending of the old and new which is my goal."

Barbara S. Bockman, born August 31, 1935, in Philadelphia, Pennsylvania, studied painting and art history at American University, and lives in Fairfax, Virginia. An artist/quiltmaker who teaches stenciling, and writes and edits on quilt subjects, Barbara's paintings, block prints, and quilts are part of private and corporate collections. Her quilts have also appeared in several publications including *Quilter's Newsletter Magazine* and *Medallion Quilts* by Jinny Beyer.

"I'd like to think my 'impact' on quilting is contributing to the resurrection of the art/craft of stenciling on fabric and combining that with piecing," she says. Barbara makes the observation that "Quiltmaking is surely the only art form one can truly get wrapped up in."

Georgia J. Bonesteel, a native of Sioux City, Iowa, and graduate of Iowa State College and Northwestern University, lives in Hendersonville, North Carolina. The creator and hostess of the television series, "Lap Quilting," she is also a teacher, lecturer, designer, shopowner, and author of *Lap Quilting with Georgia Bonesteel, More Lap Quilting,* and *New Ideas for Lap Quilting.*

Georgia feels her most important contribution to quilting is having been able, through her television series, "to show the quiltmaking process to so many people and to make them realize that they, too, have the potential to sew and create a fabric legacy." And, if more encouragement is needed, she says, "Quilters never make mistakes; we just invent new patterns."

Karen Bray was born in Denmark and came to the United States in 1923 when she was two. She lives in Walnut Creek, California, where she teaches, lectures, and writes about the pleasures of machine appliqué. Karen feels that this technique, properly done, can produce quilts beautiful enough to become family heirlooms. Several of her quilts have been featured in *Quilter's Newsletter Magazine;* and her book, *Machine Appliqué,* is in its fourth printing.

She believes enthusiasm is what gets things done. "It keeps you planning and creating and gets exciting enough to wake you from sleep to work out the next step."

Karey [Karoline] Patterson Bresenhan, born in Gilmer, Texas, lives in Houston, where she owns the quilt shop Great Expectations. Her accomplishments include being director of the International Quilt Festival since 1975, of the Quilt Market since 1979, co-director of the Texas Quilt Search, and, what she feels is most important of all, a founder of the American International Quilt Association and director of their Quilt Expo Europa, the first major international quilting conference ever held in Europe. Karey is the co-author of *Lone Stars: A Legacy of Texas Quilts, 1836-1936,* and *Hands All Around: Quilts from Many Nations.*

Of quilting and some of its motivations, she says,

". . . fragments of the world's early patchwork . . . reaffirm the timeless quality of patchwork and quilting, the certainty that men and women from earliest days have sought to combine the need for thrift with the urge to create and decorate."

Lacy Lee Folmar Bullard, of Tallahassee, Florida, was born in Minneapolis, Minnesota, and grew up in Florida. An editor and writer, she is the co-author of *Wildflowers of the Southern Coastal Plain* and *Down to Earth Vegetable Gardening Down South*, and author of *Florida Beaches* and *Arts in Florida*. Her work on quilts includes the book *Chintz Quilts: Unfading Glory* (co-author), and "The Collector: Once Out of Time," an article on the quilt collections of the Charleston (South Carolina) Museum, featured in *The Quilt Digest #3*.

Lacy feels her contribution to quilting has been the recognition that quilts made with chintz were different, and then documenting the difference in a book. "People come to quilting by many paths. It was a love of fabric that brought me there."

Hazel Carter of Vienna, Virginia, was born January 9, 1933, in Salem, Iowa, and worked for a number of years in Washington, D.C. Her grandmother taught her to quilt when she was nine, and it has remained a life-long love. Hazel's work, including several original quilt blocks, has appeared in such publications as *Lady's Circle Patchwork Quilts* and *Quilter's Newsletter Magazine*. Although she has taught, lectured, and judged, her major commitment is to The Continental Quilting Congress, founded in 1979, and The Quilters' Hall of Fame.

Speaking of The Continental Quilting Congress, Hazel says, "This convention is for the quilters, for the traditionalist and contemporary alike. It is an attempt to stretch the quilter to go a little beyond what they are doing now."

Margaret Maddox Cavigga, born October 31, 1924, in Poplar Bluff, Missouri, graduated from Louisiana State University, and did postgraduate work in art and education at the University of California, Los Angeles. Her home is in Los Angeles where she was for some years a teacher in the public schools.

Margaret, besides being the owner of the shop, The Margaret Cavigga Quilt Collection, is a historian, art consultant, appraiser of American collectibles, and quilt collector. In 1985, she donated 19 Crazy quilts, along with funds for their care and display, to the Museum of American Folk Art in New York City. Other quilt accomplishments include several articles on collecting quilts, and the book *American Antique Quilts*.

About quilts as art, Margaret M. Cavigga says, "Quilts are a true and recognized art form. What else can you buy for such a relatively reasonable amount of money that is a piece of original art with both historical value and practical use?"

Katy Christopherson, born July 8, 1921, in Hiram, Ohio, lives in Louisville, Kentucky, where she judges, writes, lectures, and teaches, as well as researches and documents old quilts. In 1981-82, Mrs. Christopherson served as consultant for the Kentucky Quilt Project, the first of the statewide searches for antique quilts. Her articles have appeared in several quilt magazines including *Lady's Circle Patchwork Quilts*, and she wrote *The Political Campaign Quilt*, a catalogue for the Kentucky Heritage Quilt Society.

As for what the ordinary quilt-lover can do about disappearing and disintegrating old quilts, Katy Christopherson says, "Find and save one quilt. If we each find a place to begin, the next decade will see a vast improvement in the care of quilts now in public hands. It is not what the volunteers *can* do for quilts, but what we *must*."

Nell Cogswell, born March 1, 1934, in Boston, Massachusetts, lives in Carlisle, Massachusetts. Her serious involvement with quilting began after three of her four children left home, and has continued to grow. Nell's work has appeared on television, the cover of a textbook, and a Hallmark puzzle, as well as in several publications including *Quilter's Newsletter Magazine* and *The Second Quiltmaker's Handbook* by Michael James.

She feels the "only constant in life is change. Without change you cannot grow. Everything you do or say alters things in some way. Hopefully for the better."

Rhoda Rudman Cohen, was born June 18, 1934, Bangor, Maine, and lives in Weston, Massachusetts. Formerly a painter, Rhoda was introduced to quilting by Nancy Halpern, with whom she occasionally collaborates. She says, "Quiltmaking is now as close as my skin. Consciously or not, everything I see, do, feel, is part of that state. It provides me with a way to express all the positive, decent things, and some indecent ones, too." Her work has appeared in several publications including *Quilter's Newsletter Magazine*, *America's Pictorial Quilts* by Caron L. Mosey, and *The Quilt Digest #3*.

About fame and its accompanying notoriety Rhoda writes:

"I am not Mt. Katahdin
I don't want tourists.
I am like martial law.
Considering groups which gather,
suspect."

Shirley Conlon of San Diego, California, was born in Patchogue, Long Island, New York, and began quilting in 1957 after discovering *The Standard Book of Quiltmaking and Collecting* by Marguerite Ickis. Her interest grew to include not only quiltmaking, but pattern collecting, research, and the compilation of an extensive bibliography on all published quilt material. She also drafted many of the patterns in Barbara Bannister's reprint booklets.

Shirley Conlon's view of quilts is that they are meant for use and comfort. "One of my fondest views is late in the evening to see the bed with a quilt on it, the lamp turned on, and a book nearby — it seems so warm and cozy and safe." About their human aspect she says, "I think just because quilts are named makes them dear and familiar. What other needlework has the final product named? Women say 'My Bear's Paw,' or 'My Double Wedding Ring,' and it's comforting."

Blanche L. Connolly, born October 23, 1934, in Jamaica Plain, Massachusetts, lives in a suburb of Boston where she was a teacher and children's librarian for many years. Since 1970, she has made quilts of traditional patterns for herself, family, and friends, as well as original wallhangings inspired by favorite poems.

"My projects often take on a life of their own," says Blanche, "the plans far outstripping the making. I won't live long enough to finish everything, but one thing is certain — I shall never be bored. Perhaps the true secret of happiness is an obsession."

Mary M. Conroy, born in Ayr, Ontario, lives in the Sudbury area where she was raised and educated. A staff educator at the Sudbury Algoma Hospital, she has also been a nurse and an alderman for the city of Sudbury, 1968-1972.

Mary's quilt accomplishments include teaching, lecturing, writing, and publishing. She is the author of *300 Years of Canada's Quilts*, and *The Complete Book of Crazy Patchwork;* was a regular contributor to *Quilter's Newsletter Magazine* in its early days; and was publisher/editor of the magazine *Canadian Quilts* from 1973 to 1982.

When asked where she fits in the quilting order of things, Mary Conroy says, "Some people are imitators — others still are adaptors. And then some of us are communicators and educators — and all of us have our place in the quilting world."

Patricia Cox was born in Minnesota, where she still lives in the city of Minneapolis. Teaching herself to quilt in the early

1960s, she has gone on to become a designer, teacher, lecturer, author, and publisher. Her books include *Log Cabin Workbook*, *Every Stitch Counts*, and *Country Children*. She also performs as a duo pianist with her husband. Among Patricia's proudest quilt accomplishments are her designs for 20th century versions of Baltimore Album Quilts, one of which translated into fabric by Bernice Eyneart, was featured in *Quilter's Newsletter Magazine* and *The Quilt Engagement Calendar 1984*.

Speaking of what quilting means to her, Patricia Cox says, "[It] has become the focus of my life, allowing me to do all the things I like to do, constantly expanding my horizons, and giving me friends all over this wonderful country."

Dorothy Cozart, a native of Oklahoma, was born on June 8, 1921, near Manchester, lives in Waukomis, and taught American folklore, and English at Phillips University. She is a quilt historian, collector, writer, and on the board of directors of the American Quilt Study Group. Dorothy's articles have been published in *Uncoverings* for 1981, 1984, and 1986, and *The Quilt Digest #5*. She feels her most important quilt-related accomplishment is the research she did for these papers, which included: American authors writing about quilts and quiltmakers, fundraising quilts, tobacco-related items in quilts, and four quilts made by a quiltmaker born in 1773.

And although Dorothy Cozart has delivered a paper and written an article she doesn't stop gathering material, for as she says, ". . . once you become interested in a subject the interest continues forever."

Carol Pinney Crabb, born September 23, 1928, in Ottawa, Kansas, lives in Columbia, Missouri, where she teaches, lectures, does research, and collects patterns and articles from old magazines and newspapers. Gems from this collection, some of which go back to 1831, have appeared from time to time in *Quilters' Journal* and *Quilter's Newsletter Magazine*.

About the deep feelings that quilts arouse in people, Carol says, "There is something about a quilt that touches the emotions of people in a way that few other objects do. I have been involved in documenting Missouri quilts. Women bring their quilts to us, holding them gently as they would a baby, and with pride in their voices say, 'I have a family heirloom.' . . . It may not be an object of great beauty to the casual observer, but to the owner it is valuable and cherished."

Sharyn Craig, born April 8, 1947, in Denver, Colorado, lives in San Diego, California. She quilts and designs, and in 1985 was named Quilt Teacher of the Year by *Professional Quilter Magazine*, who were impressed by her "emphasis on problem-solving and creativity, and her dedication to transmitting the joy of quilting." Examples of Sharyn's work and that of her students have appeared in several issues of *Quilter's Newsletter Magazine*.

Although teaching has cut into the time Sharyn Craig has for making her own quilts, she says her reward is in "watching my students become quiltmakers and knowing that, just maybe, if it weren't for me those quilts might not have been born."

Barbara Lydecker Crane, who lives in Lexington, Massachusetts, was born March 22, 1948, in Orange, New Jersey, and has a degree in fine arts from Skidmore College. Since she began seriously quilting in 1980, her work has appeared in juried and invitational shows, become part of public and private collections, and been featured in several quilt publications, including *The Quilt Engagement Calendar 1987*, *The Quilt Digest #3*, and *American Quilter*.

Barbara's approach to her work is reflected in both a personal motto, "Play attention," and this note to herself from a journal she keeps: "I hope I can always keep some sense of mystery in my art, and never become too certain about my life, either."

Mary Jo Dalrymple lives in Little Rock, Arkansas, where she was born. Originally a symphony musician who found in quilting a way to relax, it has since become a serious involvement for Mary Jo. Her work has won awards in quilt and art exhibitions, appeared in invitational shows, and been featured in several quilt publications, including a cover of *Quilter's Newsletter Magazine* and the *Quilt Art '86 Engagement Calendar.*

She says, "My specific area of interest at the moment is that zone of turbulence where the traditional meets the contemporary."

Cindy Vermillion Davis, born November 7, 1949, in Long Beach, California, graduated from the University of Southern California with degrees in elementary education, and lives on a ranch in Pagosa Springs, Colorado. Her work has appeared in several quilt publications including *Quilter's Newsletter Magazine* and *Stitch 'n Sew Quilts,* she teaches occasionally, and is co-author of *The First Mary Gibson Sampler,* a book on counted cross-stitch. Among her proudest quilt accomplishments are winning Best of Show at the Colorado State Fair for the years, 1983, 1984, and 1986.

Basically, Cindy Davis sees herself as a traditionalist with a love of bright, contrasting colors. "While I try to keep an open mind on the new quilt being developed today," she says, "I just can't help feeling that quilt design has had a Golden Age just like Greece and Rome, and when I make my own quilts my eye is much more likely to turn backwards rather than forwards."

Jean Dubois, born January 4, 1926, in Denver, Colorado, lives in Golden, Colorado. Although she has been a teacher, lecturer, publisher, quilter, and owner of a mail-order business, Jean has always considered herself primarily a writer. The author of *The Colonial History Quilt, A Galaxy of Stars: America's Favorite Quilts, Ann Orr Patchwork, Bye*

Baby Bunting, and *The Wool Quilt: Patterns and Possibilities* (called *Patchwork Quilting in Wool* in the 1985 Dover edition), she also published the quarterly newsletter *The LaPlata Review* (1981-1985), and was a regular contributor to several quilt magazines including *Quilter's Newsletter Magazine*. Her proudest quilt accomplishments are the research she did "way back in the beginning when the facts were impossible to find and even the museums didn't know what they had"; being the first international speaker to address the English Quilt Guild in Winchester, England; and the "now defunct La Plata Press."

Of creating, Jean Dubois says, "A work of art has a life of its own, timing of its own. If it balks, you have to wait. Work on it more, research it more, organize it more, think about it more, live with it longer."

Eleanor Bryant Dyson, born March 31, 1936, in Flushing, New York, lives in Annandale, Virginia. Elly, who began quilting in 1981 after years of involvement in other arts and crafts, lectures and teaches. Her original pieced picture quilts have appeared in several quilt publications, including *America's Pictorial Quilts* by Caron L. Mosey and *Quilt* magazine. She has also done a series called "The Hawaiian Muu Muu and Shirt Factory Quilts."

Of the inevitable trial-and-error process involved in quiltmaking, she says, "I guess I was lucky not coming from a quilting family because I didn't have a set of quilting rules that must be followed."

Margit Echols lives in New York City where she was born on August 25, 1944. A quiltmaker since the early 1970s, Margit teaches, designs, and writes, and in 1985 founded the Rowhouse Press. Her work includes the posters "Alphabet" and "American Sampler Quilt" (featured in *Quilter's Newsletter Magazine)*, and the books *The New American Quilt*, *The Quilter's Start-to-Finish Workbook*, and *A Patchwork Christmas*.

From her experience as both a designer and quilter, Margit feels that "trying a variation on a traditional pattern is always a good way to learn basic design principles . . . which are innate . . . and timeless."

Jean Eitel, born November 22, 1941, in Flint, Michigan, lives in North Palm Beach, Florida. She is a quiltmaker, designer, writer, teacher, lecturer, and, since 1986, the editor of *Quilt*, *Country Quilt*, and *Quilt Almanac* magazines. Her quilts have won prizes, appeared in invitational exhibits, and been featured in many publications including the *Quilt Art '85* and *'87 Engagement Calendars*.

Jean is also the author of *Creative Quiltmaking in the Mandala Tradition*, illustrator of Bettina Havig's *Missouri Heritage Quilt Book*, and contributing designer for *Creative Needlecrafts for the Home* by Linda Lindgrin.

"In response to the question is quiltmaking an art or a craft," Jean says, "We can perhaps conclude that the answer lies with each individual quiltmaker and how that individual approaches his work."

Janet B. Elwin of South Bristol, Maine, was born October 18, 1940, in Malden, Massachusetts, growing up in nearby Somerville. A quiltmaker since 1972, Janet teaches, designs, writes, lectures, runs a business, and was one of the founders of The New England Quilters' Guild (1976) as well as an initiator of their museum in Lowell, Massachusetts (1987). Her quilts, including personal favorites, "The Good Earth," "The Little Fishes," "Winter Solstice," and "Ocean Odyssey," have been widely exhibited and appeared in such publications as *Quilter's Newsletter Magazine* and *Quilting*. She is also the author of *Ode to Grandmother* and *Hexagon Magic*.

Janet feels that it's "fatal to put away an unfinished quilt. Always keep it in eye's view just so it can beckon to you, 'FINISH ME.' "

Helen M. Ericson, a native Kansan who lives in Emporia, was born June 26, 1929, in Elk County, received her first seven years of education in a one-room schoolhouse, and has a degree in home economics from Emporia State University. Besides having made over 125 quilts, many of them prizewinners, Helen teaches, lectures, writes, researches, and is one of two Master Folk Artists in Kansas, an apprentice program funded by the National Endowment for the Arts. Her work appears often in quilt magazines such as *Lady's Circle Patchwork Quilts,* and she does a column for the *Baldwin (Kansas) Ledger.*

In 1970, Helen purchased the mail order business Mrs. Danner's Quilts from Scioto Imhoff Danner (1891-1975), and in continuing to provide patterns in the spirit of Mrs. Danner, one of the famous names of the 1930s quilt revival, has maintained a living link with quilt history. Other accomplishments include revising and republishing the *Danner Quilt Pattern Catalogs,* #1-4, doing new volumes, #6-7, and writing, with Betty J. Hagerman (1923-1986), *The 1978 Kansas Quilt Symposium Catalog.*

When people ask Helen which is her favorite quilt, she answers, "That is like asking me which was the favorite of my children? Each quilt has its charms, its problems, its uses, its joys. . . . "

Dorothy S. Finley, born July 25, 1929, in Grand Junction, Tennessee, lives in Memphis. Her interest in quilting began in 1974 when illness forced an early retirement. Of the many quilts Dorothy has made since then, her proudest achievement has been the design and execution of "Dot's Vintage 1983." This quilt not only won the first Gingher Award for Workmanship in the American Quilting Society's premier show (1985), but also earned Dorothy her Master's Certification from the National Quilting Association's Master's Guild, making her the second NQA member to be thus honored. Numerous quilt publications including *Quilter's Newsletter Magazine* and the *Quilt Art '88 Engagement Calendar* have featured her work.

In speaking of how she came to be a master quiltmaker, Dorothy Finley says, "I'm a self-taught quilter. I learned by reading and doing. I used the trial-and-error method with lots of errors."

Judy Florence, a native of Wisconsin, was born April 30, 1945, in Waupaca, has degrees in liberal arts, home economics education, and adult education from the University of Wisconsin, and lives in Eau Claire. A quilter, designer, teacher, lecturer, and author, Judy's quilts have been widely exhibited, appeared in needlecraft publications, and been featured in her books *Award-Winning Quilts and How to Make Them*, *Award-Winning Quilts: Book II*, *Award-Winning Scrap Quilts*, and *Award-Winning Quick Quilts*. "Computer Kaleidoscope," one of the results of designing with her computer, can be seen in the *Quilt Art '85 Engagement Calendar*.

From her own experience, Judy Florence observes, "Quilting has come to have heightened meaning for me when I began to make quilts that were not somebody else's designs, quilts that were uniquely mine. After several years of quilting, I made a quilt for my son, incorporating elements from his distinct ethnic background. That quilt, 'Iroquois,' was the first one into which I put not only my hands and head, but also my heart."

Marianne Fons, born June 27, 1949, in Des Moines, Iowa, graduated with degrees in literature from Drake University, and lives at Meadowlark Farm, Winterset, Iowa. A quilter, designer, lecturer, and writer, Marianne is co-author of *Classic Quilted Vests* and *Classic Basket Patterns*, and author of *Fine Feathers*. Her work, including the story, "Crazy Quilt," featured in *The Quilt Digest#3*, has appeared in several publications, and she helped compile the *Quilt Cottage Cookbook*. One of her proudest accomplishments is "The Lady Liberty Medallion Quilt," winner from Iowa in The Great American Quilt Contest, 1986.

In speaking of words to live by, Marianne Fons says, "The

sustaining philosophy of my life has been 'the more you give, the more you get back.' "

Helen Young Frost, born May 16, 1952, in Salt Lake City, Utah, and raised in California, lives in Arizona. She lectures, teaches, collects antique quilts, and with her mother, Blanche Young, wrote and published *The Lone Star Quilt Handbook* (the result of six years of teaching and "refining"), *Trip Around the World Quilts*, *The Flying Geese Quilt*, and *The Boston Commons Quilt.* Helen hopes these books with their "easier ways for making some traditional designs will have encouraged people to make quilts that they might not have otherwise."

For Helen Young Frost, ". . . quilts feed the soul. If we just wanted warmth we would buy a blanket, if we wanted color . . . a bedspread, but we need something more."

Donna Duchesne Garofalo, born June 15, 1949, in Hartford, Connecticut, lives in Chaplin, Connecticut. Learning to quilt with friends several years ago, Donna's first original piece, "Mom, The Quilt's Falling," was inspired by a vivid dream, and won Best of Show at the Eastern States Exposition Great Quilt Festival in Springfield, Massachusetts, 1983. Since then, Donna's work has won many other awards and been featured in several issues of *Quilter's Newsletter Magazine.* This has included pieces from the "quilt within a quilt" series and the "seashore" series. Donna says that "working in a series is a good way to fully explore an idea."

Flavin Williams Glover, born October 31, 1951, in Cullman, Alabama, lives in Auburn, Alabama. She is a quilter, designer, teacher, and lecturer whose landscape quilts done in variations of Log Cabin piecing have been featured in numerous quilt publications, including *Quilter's Newsletter Magazine*, *Quiltmakers Calendar 1983*, and *Great American Quilts of 1987.*

When asked what she considered her most important quilt-related accomplishment, Flavin said, "My best thing in quilting is yet to come."

Mary Golden, who was born June 15, 1945, in Des Moines, Iowa, divides her time between summers in Gloucester, Massachusetts, and schooltime in New Hampton, New Hampshire. A teacher, designer, and writer, Mary's quilt career began in 1972 with the repair of an old family quilt. Her quilts can be seen on the walls of homes, hospitals, and businesses, and in many publications, including *Stitch 'n Sew Quilts* and *Quilter's Newsletter Magazine*. She is the author of *The Yankee Friendship Quilt Book*. Mary considers her most important quilt-related accomplishments to be the part she played as a Founding Mother of the New England Quilters' Guild, and the development — over many years and through countless workshops — of the kaleidoscope block with its infinite variations. Her favorite quilt is "Ne'er Encounter Pain," made while her husband recovered from serious surgery, and later purchased by the American Quilter's Society for their museum.

Mary Golden believes a "special language exists among quiltmakers. Their words and thoughts are expressed in the patterns, fabrics, quilting designs, and colors that they use in their quilts. To know their quilts is to understand them in a special way."

Irene Goodrich, born June 4, 1926, in Wyethville, Virginia, lives in Columbus, Ohio, where she teaches, does some collecting, and has a business in her home. Her first love, however, is quilting, and she especially enjoys entering a competition. Irene's work has appeared in several quilt publications, including *American Quilter* and *Quilt* magazines, and many of her over 48 quilts have taken top prizes in shows throughout the country. Among her proudest accomplishments are winning first place in the 1983 Stearns and Foster quilt contest with "Trumpet Vine," and having the

American Quilter's Society purchase "Lancaster County Rose" for their museum.

And of those prize-winning quilts, Irene Goodrich says, "I will not sacrifice good workmanship for speed. It frustrates me that doing a quilt is so time-consuming, but I haven't found a way yet to speed the process and have a first-class quilt."

Ruth Green, born August 7, 1933, in Negaunee, Michigan, lives in Rancho Palos Verdes, California. An accomplished pianist who taught music for many years, she is owner/operator of the business Ruth Green The Handylady. Ruth began quilting in the early 1970s and has since been coordinator and main needleperson for several group quilts, as well as making quilts for family and special friends. Her favorite quilt "to keep" is a "Sunbonnet Sue Friendship Quilt" that includes the names of friends and five generations of family. She hopes some descendant will add to it when she's gone.

In speaking of her personal philosophy, Ruth says, "I must remind myself that I cannot solve all the problems of the world, but if the influence of my life on those about me is positive, then they in turn will more likely have happier, more productive lives and be a force for good in the world."

Sheila Minkin Groman, born March 10, 1942, in Hollywood, California, lives in Chelmsford, Massachusetts. She is a quiltmaker, lecturer, teacher, designer, avid gardener, and a student of fashion design whose work has appeared in such publications as *Quilt* and *Quilter's Newsletter Magazine*. Of her many quilts, Sheila's own favorites include "Patches of Lilies," "Mishkan Star," and "Miss Liberty." Another quilt, "This Year in Jerusalem of Gold," made to honor son Kevin's Bar Mitzvah in Israel, was stolen from an exhibit in 1984 and never recovered. Although a quilt, like anything of human value, is irreplaceable, Sheila made a "sister quilt," "Remember Jerusalem," in 1987.

Of her work, Sheila Groman says, "I guess my quilts are too expressive of traditional flavor to be considered 'contemporary,' and too modern or unusual to be considered 'traditional.' But that's all right with me, because labels are sometimes limiting and I love the rhythm and symmetry in traditional work and the newness and excitement in contemporary work. I feel good that my quilting seems to reflect both areas."

Joyce Gross, a native Californian who lives in Mill Valley, was born August 11, 1924, in Alameda. Her quilt accomplishments include teaching, lecturing, writing, leading seminars and study groups, coordinating workshops, serving as special consultant on the film *The Hardman Quilt: Portrait of an Age* (1975), and editing and publishing *Quilters' Journal*. This last, a periodical founded in 1977 for the quilt scholar, historian, and enthusiast, is regarded by Joyce as her most important contribution to quilting. In writing and researching many of the articles, she has brought to light the lives of some of the 20th century's most talented quiltmakers.

Speaking of *Quilters' Journal*, Joyce Gross sees it as a by-product of her passion for collecting historical items. "My house runneth over. Fortunately, I don't have to clean as much because it is full of, not 'stuff,' but items of historical significance."

Genevieve Pilgrim Guracar, born February 3, 1936, in Chicago, Illinois, lives in Mountain View, California. A teacher, designer, needlewoman, and cartoonist who uses her talents in behalf of her convictions, Genevieve designed and coordinated the "Signature Peace Quilt," "The People's Bicentennial Quilt," "The Women in Struggle Quilt," and "Visions." "The Women in Struggle Quilt" has been exhibited throughout the United States and internationally from Kenya to Sweden and Ecuador to Greenham Common, England.

Her cartoons, under the name of bulbul (in Turkish poetry, a bird of protest), have appeared in peace, labor, feminist, and environmental publications.

bulbul — Genevieve Guracar — says:

Beth Gutcheon, born March 18, 1945, in Sewickley, Pennsylvania, lives in New York City. She began teaching in the early 1970 s and has been a quiltmaker, teacher, lecturer, designer, and writer whose work has appeared in numerous publications including *Lady's Circle Patchwork Quilts*, *Quilter's Newsletter Magazine*, and *The Second Quiltmaker's Handbook* by Michael James. Beth is the author of *The Perfect Patchwork Primer*, *The Quilt Design Workbook* (co-author), and the novels *The New Girls* and *Still Missing*. The latter was made into the movie *Without a Trace*, for which she wrote the screenplay.

In speaking of quiltmaking, Beth Gutcheon offers this approach: "To make function and necessity a positive good, to start with what must be and evolve it into a truly original design style that suits our life and times, is a real and important challenge, one that must be respected if quiltmaking is to be a living art as well as a heritage craft."

Jeffrey Gutcheon lives in New York City where he was born January 3, 1941. He has degrees in English and architecture, and careers in music, architecture, quilting, and textile design. The career in quilting has encompassed quiltmaking, teaching, lecturing, writing, the designing and manufacturing of fabrics, and a business, Gutcheon Patchworks. His quilts have appeared in many publications including *Lady's Circle Patchwork Quilts* and the *Quiltmakers 1986* calendar; he is co-author of *The Quilt Design Workbook*, author of *Diamond Patchwork*, and writes the column "Not for Shopkeepers Only," a feature of *Quilter's Newsletter Magazine* since 1981. Jeffrey feels his most important quilting accomplishment has been the production of the American Classic Line of Fabrics, while "Judy in Arabia" (1974) and "Crystal Mountain" (1978) are among his favorite quilts.

Of quiltmaking and its future, Jeffrey Gutcheon says, "Now is the time for teaching technique as the fundamental tool of craftsmanship and allowing style to remain a personal consideration. In the service of quiltmaking's future, good teachers today should seek diligently to expand their students' horizons rather than narrowing them, and that means treating all the contributions to quiltmaking over the last decade with equal respect."

Ernest Byron Haight lives on the farm in David City, Nebraska, where he was born, July 20, 1899. A farmer and engineer, who graduated Phi Beta Kappa from the University of Nebraska in 1924, Ernest's quiltmaking began with a challenge from his wife, Isabelle Hooper Haight, a fine quilter in her own right. Since that day in 1935, he has made over 300 quilts, many of which have received awards, been widely exhibited, and appeared in publications such as *Quilter's Newsletter Magazine* and *The Complete Book of Machine Quilting* by Robbie and Tony Fanning. He has also written and published *Practical Machine Quilting for the Homemaker* (1974), and was inducted into the Nebraska Quilter's Hall of Fame, July 1986.

From years of experience in making quilts on a domestic sewing machine, Ernest B. Haight offers this advice for success: "Accuracy is the key . . . the parts must be very carefully drawn and cut . . . and the quiltmaker must train their sewing machine for very accurate seams."

Jan Halgrimson, born July 18, 1935, in Renton, Washington, lives in nearby Edmonds. A quiltmaker, author, and publisher, Jan's books include *Scraps Can Be Beautiful*, *Great Scrap Bag Quilts*, and *Patching Things Up*. The three books, published by her own Weaver-Finch Publications, comprise a collection of over 360 patterns, some original, plus brief commentary.

Jan Halgrimson says, "The most important aspect of creating from scraps is . . . the sentimental value of a quilt made from scraps. A quilt made from your baby's clothing will become more dear as the years pass."

Nancy Halpern, born December 5, 1938, in Boston, Massachusetts, lives in nearby Natick. She studied at Radcliffe College, the University of California, Berkeley (from which she has a degree in English), and the Boston Architectural Center. Nancy, who began teaching quilting in 1973, is also a lecturer, writer, and designer, but she considers herself first and foremost a quiltmaker. Her quilts have been widely exhibited, are part of private and corporate collections, and have been featured in numerous quilt publications including *The Second Quiltmaker's Handbook* by Michael James; *The Quilt Digest #4; Hands All Around: Quilts From Many Nations* by Robert Bishop, Karey P. Bresenhan, and Bonnie Leman; and *Quilter's Newsletter Magazine*.

Nancy Halpern's reply to what she considered her favorite and/or most important quilt-related accomplishment was, "Since I started making my first quilt, my life and work have become so interrelated this question is impossible to answer —

I cut, I breathe —
I sew, I teach —
I quilt, I smile."

LaVonne R. Hanlon, born May 9, 1938, in Scottdale, Pennsylvania, lives in Laurel, Maryland. An active member of the National Quilting Association in its early years and a guiding light of their publication, *Patchwork Patter,* her work has appeared in several quilt magazines including *Lady's Circle Patchwork Quilts* and *Quilt World.*

LaVonne says, "I enjoy creating quilts that record history. '200 Years: Flags and Fashions' (1976) commemorates America's bicentennial, while 'Family Album Chain,' made from scraps saved by my mother and me in the 1940s to 1970s is a family history." When first shown in 1977, this quilt was criticized for its use of liquid embroidery combined with embroidery, but in 1986, after stenciling had become popular, it won a Viewer's Choice Award. Among LaVonne's other quilts are "Double Polish Chain," honoring her father's family, and "Precious Biblical Moments," inspired while grieving the loss of her oldest son in 1985.

Sember Hartman, born December 14, 1946, in Geneva, Illinois, lives in Conklin, New York. Before becoming seriously involved in quilting, she was a painter in oils and acrylics (her environmental paintings can be seen at the Broome County Natural Science Museum, Binghamton, New York). Sember teaches, exhibits, writes, designs, and makes quilted clothing, as well as being a quiltmaker who does 14-stitches-to-the-inch quilting. Her work has appeared in many publications including *American Quilter,* and she is a contributing editor for *Quilt World Magazine* with her column, "Quilting in the Corner," a feature since 1981.

About those 14-stitches-to-the-inch, Sember Hartman says, "For this quilter, the most important aspect of quiltmaking is the very act of quilting, of changing a flat graphic design into a three-dimensional work. The miracle of quilting is what keeps me designing and making assorted tops."

Sarah Hass, born on a farm in Union County, Iowa, lives in Fort Madison, Iowa. She grew up in the 1920s and '30s, attending three colleges, including the University of Northern Iowa from which she has a degree in art education. Sarah made her first quilt when she was 12, but it was the experience of winning prizes and recognition for three designs in 1975 that "awakened in me the exciting truth that not all the patchwork designs in the world had been invented. In fact . . . I realized the great body of designs was yet to come." Since then she has won prizes for her original designs as well as marketed them. Her work has appeared in several quilt publications including *America's Pictorial Quilts* by Caron L. Mosey and *Quilter's Newsletter Magazine*.

An important event in Sarah's quilting life was a 1986 trip to the Philippines during which she gave the presentations "Quilting," "Quilting, The American Heritage," and "Quilts as Art." She considers her most significant quilt-related accomplishment as coming "to recognize the fact that my 'bent' toward creativity is not only a vital part of what I am, but it is also a very worthy quality."

Carla J. Hassel, born September 11, 1948, in Michigan City, Indiana, lives in Des Moines, Iowa. A teacher, lecturer, author, quiltmaker, and designer, Carla's classroom experiences led her to write *You Can Be a Super Quilter* and *Super Quilter II*. Two years as a volunteer coordinator for the Hmong-Lao Foundation was the inspiration for a third book, *Creating Pa Ndau Appliqué*, as well as for the art piece, "Covenant," funded by a grant from Iowa State University. Her work has also appeared in several quilt publications including *Lady's Circle Patchwork Quilts*.

And who makes quilts? Carla J. Hassel says, "There is no universal quilter. We are young, we are old. We have taught ourselves, we have spent fortunes on books and classes. We are traditionalists, we are designers. We are mathematicians, we can't add two plus two . . . We use precious scraps, we buy by the bolt. Yet there is common ground. We have phenomenal energy and unswerving determination. We record our lives in fabrics and stitches."

Sandra L. Hatch who lives in Newton, New Hampshire, was born August 19, 1948, in Lincoln, Maine, the oldest of six girls. She graduated from the University of Maine with a degree in home economics, and feels her mother and grandmother's needlework talents plus her own involvement in 4-H were important in making her the person she is today. She made her first quilt, a Crazy quilt, when she was 10, and "the completion of any quilt project continues to be a major cause of celebration for me." She taught school for several years before becoming editor of the magazines *Quilt World Omnibook* (1982), *Quilt World* (1986) and *Stitch 'n Sew Quilts* (1987).

Of her life, Sandra Hatch says, "I manage to edit the magazines, quilt some, spend time with my family, and keep my house relatively clean. I am what I consider an average working mother. I am extremely happy with my family, my work, and my life right now, and I hope it lasts forever."

Bettina Havig, originally from Kansas City, has a degree in math and physics from the University of Missouri, did graduate work at Tulane University, and lives in Columbia, Missouri. A teacher, lecturer, and quilt historian who began quilting in 1970, Bettina's articles have appeared in *Quilters' Journal*, *Missouri Journal of Folklife*, and *Uncoverings 1985*. From 1977 to 1985 she was the owner/operator of the Quilt Cottage, one of Missouri's first quilt specialty shops. She considers having been director of the Missouri Heritage Quilt Project her most important quilt-related accomplishment. This experience also resulted in her book, *Missouri Heritage Quilts*.

Bettina says, "Quiltmaking is my true passion — all of us need to find an expression of faith in the future."

Dixie Haywood, born May 6, 1933, in Seattle, Washington, lives in Pensacola, Florida, where she is a writer, designer, teacher, lecturer, and quiltmaker. Her proudest quilt accomplishments include two books, *The Contemporary Crazy Quilt Project Book* and *Crazy Quilting With a Difference (Crazy Quilt Patchwork* in the Dover edition), as well as "the students I have taught, the quilts I have made, the guilds I have helped found, and the articles I have written." Dixie's work, both written and quilted, has appeared in numerous publications such as *Lady's Circle Patchwork Quilts* and *Quilt World.*

She believes that "because quilts are both functional and go beyond function, they have a timeless, transcendental quality that links us to past and future."

Dolores A. Hinson, born September 10, 1930, in Jamestown, New York, lives in Austin, Texas. A lecturer, teacher, designer, quiltmaker, historian, and author, she is especially proud of having been, in the 1950s, one of the early nurturers and promoters of the mid-20th century quilt renaissance. Dolores was also one of the founders of the National Quilting Association (1970). Her books include *A Quilting Manual, A Quilter's Companion, A Second Quilter's Companion, Quilts for Babies and Children, American Graphic Designs*, and *The Sunbonnet Family of Quilt Patterns.*

Dolores Hinson, who has suffered much ill-health in her lifetime and can take none of her days for granted, says, "Each sunrise is a gift and each sunset a triumph."

Joseph F. Hollingshead, who lives in Kennewick, Washington, was born October 30, 1912, in Shelby County, Tennessee, growing up in the Mississippi River delta country, witness to a now-vanished world. His working life ran the gamut from picking cotton to a job in an atomic energy plant, and took him all over the United States. Joe's first quilt was made in 1934 to prove to a girlfriend he could utilize the scraps of material she thought too small to keep. Since then, working for his own creative satisfaction and the pleasure and comfort of his family, he has become a master of the Postage Stamp Picture quilt. Some of these quilts are "Ye Olde Kitchen" (23,000 pieces), "Steamboat 'Round the Bend" (27,530 pieces), and "The Little People's Quilt Festival" (30,205 pieces). His work has appeared in *Quilter's Newsletter Magazine* and the *Quiltmakers 1986* calendar.

For one of his great-granddaughters, Joseph Hollingshead wrote, and then pieced into her quilt, the following verse:

"A billowy grey cloud in the sky
Threatens to rain by and by
A peal of thunder on the wind
A steamboat wails around the bend.

Wild geese honk upon the wing
A noisy crow presumes to sing
Cozy 'neath this pastoral scene
A sleepyhead prepares to dream."

Doris Hoover of Palo Alto, California, was born 1927 in Fort Payne, Alabama, and grew up in Chattanooga, Tennessee, where she graduated as an art major from the University of Tennessee. A teacher, lecturer, writer, and quiltmaker, Doris has exhibited in the United States and abroad. Her work has been featured in several publications including *Quilter's Newsletter Magazine* and *The Complete Book of Machine Quilting* by Robbie and Tony Fanning, and she is the co-author of *Tassels*. A life-long interest in wings and feathers is reflected in two of her favorite quilts, "As a Hen Gathers Her Brood," and "In the Shadow of His Wing" (owned by the North Carolina Museum of Art, Raleigh).

On being an artist and a person, Doris Hoover says, "I create because I want to, or perhaps more truly because I am compelled to by some inner force. . . . My goals are not specific except that I want to keep in touch with what and who I am, and where I come from, and to trust my own perceptions."

Margaret Horton, born in Nottingham, England, on Christmas Day, came to the United States in 1957 and lives in Atlanta, Georgia. Although she actually learned to sew at her mother's knee, Margaret's first quilt was made some years later as a new bride in World War II England. Since then she has taught extensively, designed projects, and written articles for various needlework publications, including the column "Quilts of the South," a regular feature of *Quilt World Omnibook* since 1982.

And in this limerick Margaret Horton takes a look at a "Quilter's Revenge":

"There was a young woman called Clyde
Whose sweetheart deserted the bride.
    Right after the jilt
    She stitched him a quilt
But left pins right inside the inside."

Roberta Horton, who lives in Berkeley, California, was born in Schenectady, New York, and grew up in California. Roberta, who sees herself as a quiltmaking teacher, lecturer, and author, began teaching in 1972, and the theme quilts she developed and made with her classes were featured in several issues of *Quilter's Newsletter Magazine.* The author of *Stained Glass Quilting Technique, An Amish Adventure*, and *Calico and Beyond,* she also served as consultant for the Sunset book *Quilting, Patchwork and Appliqué.*

And for all those quilters with their hoards of fabric, Roberta Horton has these encouraging words: ". . . I have finally come to realize it's an unrealistic goal to use up all the fabric I own. It's enough that a fabric sparks my creativity, whether or not I actually use it in a project."

Carter G. Houck, born May 2, 1924, in Washington, D.C., graduated from the Commonwealth University of Virginia, and lives in New York City. She has been the editor of

Lady's Circle Patchwork Quilts since its second issue in 1974, and is the author of many books including *American Quilts and How to Make Them, The Boat Buff's Book of Embroidery* (both with Myron Miller), *All Flags Flying* (with Robert Bishop), and *The Patchwork Pattern Book*.

Carter says, "I wish I could lay claim to having made a quilt as beautiful as those that we photograph — alas, my typewriter does not turn out quilts! Perhaps I have been able to encourage other quilters and to broaden the view of many, especially those who feel that there is a great gulf between the 'traditional' and 'art' quilts."

Marion L. Huyck, born January 25, 1943, in St. Joseph, Michigan, lives in Evanston, Illinois, and has considered herself a professional quilter since 1982. Her work has been widely exhibited and featured in numerous quilting publications including *American Quilter* and the *Quilt Art '85 Engagement Calendar*. When asked what she considered her most important quilt-related accomplishments, Marion said, ". . . the quilts themselves, the 'best' always being the one I am making now. It is the process of making quilts that excites me most. I am proud of 'The Russian Medallion,' of 'Crocuses,' of 'Nothing Gold Can Stay,' and of 'October' . . . but I am also grateful that I have room in my life for my family, for many books, for volunteering at school, for learning about particle physics, and planting gardens."

Speaking of her life now, Marion Huyck observes, "Here at the midpoint of my life, I find myself confronting each day as a series of decisions to make, and the question is always whether I will make the 'right' decision in each case, all the time reminding myself that I am boundlessly lucky to have a choice at all."

Lois K. Ide, born June 3, 1920, in Swanton, Ohio, graduated from the Toledo Hospital School of Nursing, and lives in Bucyrus, Ohio. A quiltmaker, teacher, writer, and collector whose work has appeared in many quilting publications including *The Quilt Engagement Calendar 1986* and *America's Pictorial Quilts* by Caron L. Mosey, Lois made her first quilt in 1941. Of the many since then, her favorites are "Thimble Anthology," "Amish Lancaster Rose," "Liberty, The Crucible of Freedom," and "The Monkey and The Leopard." Her most important quilt-related accomplishment, she feels, has been "to open the eyes of young quilters as to their true creative abilities. This goes far beyond the teaching of how-to techniques."

Speaking of her preference in quilts, Lois says, "There are only two kinds of pie my husband enjoys — hot or cold. As for me there are only two kinds of quilts I like — old or new."

John Rice Irwin, born December 11, 1930, at the home of his grandfather Rice in Knox County, Tennessee, lives in Norris, Tennessee, where he grew up. A graduate of Lincoln Memorial University, he also has a degree in international law from the University of Tennessee, and after a career in education devotes himself full time to his Museum of Appalachia, Norris, Tennessee.

John Rice is considered a leading authority on the history, culture, and music of the Southern Appalachian region, and has lectured and written extensively on these subjects. Included among his many books is *A People and Their Quilts,* the research for which gave him the opportunity to record "so many great quilters . . . from the Southern Appalachian Mountains." Of quilting in this area he says, "When the quilt revival began sweeping the country, the art-craft had to be resurrected in most areas, but it never died here. This region provides a glimpse into a lifestyle related to quilts that no longer exists in more urbanized, industrialized and less isolated regions."

Michael James, born June 30, 1949, in New Bedford, Massachusetts, has degrees in fine arts from Southeastern Massachusetts University and the Rochester Institute of

Technology, and lives in Somerset Village, Massachusetts. A quiltmaker, teacher, lecturer, writer, and leader of workshops on design and color, Michael's quilts have been widely exhibited, both in the United States and abroad, and many are part of private and corporate collections. His work appears in numerous publications, including *The Quilt Digest #1*, and *The Art Quilt* by Michael Kile and Penny McMorris, and he is the author of *The Quiltmaker's Handbook*, and *The Second Quiltmaker's Handbook.*

Speaking of one of the universal problems of the artist, Michael James says, "It is easier to please than to challenge and stimulate."

Jean V. Johnson, born May 22, 1931, in Baltimore, Maryland, lives in Olathe, Kansas. A quiltmaker and teacher who made her first quilt in 1957, Jean began working with her own representational designs in 1979, exploring and expanding the possibilities of strip-piecing, the hexagon, and curved patches. Her quilts have been exhibited widely, appear on the walls of private homes and public buildings, and been featured in numerous publications including *America's Pictorial Quilts*, by Caron L. Mosey, and *Quilt Art '86 Engagement Calendar.*

"Quiltmaking has enhanced my life in an incredible way," says Jean. "I meet people of all ages everywhere who share a common love affair with fabric, needle and thread, tired eyes, sore fingers, and beauty."

Helen Kelley, born Helen Louise Longfield on April 28, 1927, in Englewood, New Jersey, lives in Minneapolis, Minnesota. A quiltmaker for much of her life, some of Helen's better-known quilts include "Mother Goose," "Litle Fairy Tale House," "Norwegian Elves," "Thou Beside Me Singing in the Wilderness," and "Unicorn." She teaches, lectures, and writes, and her work has appeared in numerous publications including *The Quilt Engagement Calendar* for 1984 and 1986. Other accomplishments are the column "Loose

Threads," *A Quilter's Newsletter Magazine* feature since 1981, and the book *Scarlet Ribbons*.

Helen Kelley has this advice, not just for the quilter, but for Everyperson: "Don't ever measure yourself by what the next person is doing. Whatever his speed or ability or vision it has nothing to do with you. What does have to do with you is that you fulfill your own vision in your own way."

U Khin, born April 21, 1911, in Pegu, Burma, received a degree in general science from the University of Rangoon, retired from a career as an educator, and lives in Bethesda, Maryland. He began making quilts in 1970 after his wife Yvonne became a quiltmaker, and is now as devoted a practitioner as she. Most of U's quilts are original designs, and his 10-12 quilting-stitches-to-an-inch can be found on all of his quilts and some of Yvonne's. He also collects quilts, paints, and is a frequent contributor to magazines such as *Quilt* and *Quilt World Omnibook*.

For those quilters who become discouraged about the amount of time quilting requires, U Khin offers this original proverb: "A quilt top is in a transition on the way to becoming a lovely quilt with a few minutes a day of quilting."

Yvonne M. Khin, born in Prome, Burma, and a graduate of Burma Commercial College in Rangoon, lives in Bethesda, Maryland. Her career, until her retirement in 1981, included working for the British Ministry of Information in India and China during World War II, and for the International Monetary Fund in Washington, D.C. Yvonne's needlework education began in kindergarten and continued on through high school, but her first quilt was not made until the late 1950s as a gift for an aunt in chilly Scotland. Her quilts have since appeared in many quilt publications including *America's Glorious Quilts* by Dennis Duke and Deborah Harding, and been the subject of numerous magazine articles by her husband, U Khin. Other accomplishments include the book *The Collector's Dictionary of Quilt Names and Patterns,* and the quilt, "Miss Liberty," winner from Maryland in The Great American Quilt Contest (1985).

Yvonne Khin thinks that "Quilts — any kind of quilts — are expressive of their time and each is created for a purpose. A collection of quilts is therefore like a history book that reveals much more information than meets the eye."

Roderick Kiracofe, born April 8, 1951, in Huntington, Indiana, lives in San Francisco, California. He is responsible for bringing together the quilts in the "Showcase" section of each *The Quilt Digest,* a skillful compilation of classical, contemporary, traditional, and experimental.

Roderick feels his most important quilt-related accomplishments to date are ". . . producing and designing *Yvonne Porcella: A Colorful Book* . . . organizing and designing an exhibition of doll quilts and related objects in Tokyo, December 1985, and starting *The Quilt Digest* with Michael Kile."

Mary Louise Kitsen, born June 30, 1929, in Bristol, Connecticut, grew up in Plainville, Connecticut, and lives in nearby Plantsville. A writer who sold her first work at 15 and has been a newspaper reporter and feature editor, Mary Louise is a full-time free-lancer doing everything from Sunday School material to articles for *The Ladies' Home Journal.* Among her favorite assignments are reviews of live performances and interviews with performers. She is known to quilters for her "Quilts in History" and "The Heritage of Quilts" columns that appeared for many years in *Quilt World* and *Quilt World Omnibook.*

And you don't have to make quilts to love and appreciate them, for as Mary Louise Kitsen says, "My mother still makes magnificent quilts, as did my grandmother, great-grandmother, and great-great-grandmother . . . I write about quilts. I'm absolutely terrible with a needle."

Joanne Kost, a native of Connecticut, was born November 24, 1943, in New Britain, has a degree in fine arts from the University of Hartford, and lives in Sandy Hook. A quiltmaker, designer, lecturer, and teacher, Joanne attributes her artistic talents to a creative family. Her work has been exhibited in juried and invitational shows, and been featured in many issues of *Quilter's Newsletter Magazine*. Patterns of her designs are marketed through Leman Publications.

Joanne says, "My aim has been to create quilts that are not only decorative and meaningful, but that say something about me."

Bee Neeley Kuckelman, born October 12, 1925, in El Dorado, Kansas, lives in Columbia, Missouri. A quiltmaker, writer, and amateur astronomer, Bee's accomplishments include a one-woman quilt show, appearances in *Quilter's Newsletter Magazine*, and a book of quilting poems, *Keep Me in Stitches*. She is especially proud of the quilts she has made for each of her nine children, and of acting as a liaison between non-quilters with family quilt tops, and quilters who can finish these heirlooms.

In this verse from her poem "Starry Starry Quilt," Bee conveys the wonderful feeling that only sleeping under a quilt can bring:

"No matter if it's raining out,
or snow is three feet deep,
the weather will not bother me.
Beneath the stars I'll sleep."

Edward Larson, born July 28, 1931, in Joplin, Missouri, lives in Libertyville, Illinois. He is well known for story quilts of a bright, folk art-like quality, and although he does not sew himself, he makes the patterns, selects the fabrics, and finds a quiltmaker to turn his designs into reality. Ed also makes wind toys and painted wooden sculptures, teaches, and lectures. His work has been widely exhibited and appears in numerous publications including *America's*

Pictorial Quilts by Caron L. Mosey, *The Quilt Digest #3*, and *The Quilt Engagement Calendar 1979*.

Of his quilt-related accomplishments, Ed feels the most important are the workshops he gives on making story quilts: "This is a chance to share some wonderful lives in the construction of the quilt, because a picture quilt is often a story about someone's life."

Jean Ray Laury was born and grew up in Doon, Iowa, graduated from Northern Iowa University with a degree in art and education, has a master's from Stanford University in design, and lives in Clovis, California. Her first quilt, made as part of her master's project, led to an article in *House Beautiful* magazine in 1960. Jean's work since then has appeared in numerous publications such as *Family Circle* magazine and *America's Glorious Quilts* by Dennis Duke and Deborah Harding, been widely exhibited, and commissioned for the walls of various businesses. Other accomplishments include the column "Talking It Over," a regular feature of *Quilter's Newsletter Magazine* since 1984; many books, ranging from the early *Appliqué Stitchery* and *Quilts and Coverlets: A Contemporary Approach* to the humorous Sunbonnet Sue series; and teaching, lecturing, designing, and judging. One of her most valuable achievements is *The Creative Woman's Getting-It-All-Together-at-Home Handbook*, a book that has given support and encouragement to thousands of women.

Speaking of finding the time for what is important, Jean Ray Laury says, "Needs, responsibilities, and demands seem always to exceed the available time. That's when we must consciously select, choosing how we'll spend the limited hours, and this selection gives evidence to our priorities, whether or not they are consciously stated."

Millie Leathers, of Vernon, Indiana, was born May 24, 1933, in Red Boiling Springs, Tennessee. Although she made her first quilt block at four and had a career in needlework, Millie did not become a serious quilter until 1973. Since then she has taught, lectured, judged, coordinated quilt shows, and been responsible for her shop, Hoosier Patchwork. Other accomplishments include serving as Quilt and Textile Director of the Jennings County Historical Society Museum, and founding, as well as being on the board of directors of, the Indiana Quilt Registry. Millie also publishes original quilt and folk toy patterns, is the co-author of *Stitching a Legacy*, and author of *Bears, Quilts and Other Little Luvs, Indiana Legacy, First, Nine and Always*, and *Sugar and Spice*. Her work has appeared in several quilt magazines including *American Quilter*.

Of the importance of craftsmanship, Millie Leathers says, "The way a person learns needlework can mean the difference not only in skills, but also in appreciation. The American heritage of needlecrafts is rich today because of the strict teachings of another time. It was a code of ethics passed from generation to another."

Paula Lederkramer, who was born March 30, 1932, in New York City, has lived all her life in the metropolitan area, making her home in nearby Levittown. Although Paula has no formal art training, she comes from a background of artistic people and has always been interested in traditional needlecrafts. Her first attempt at quiltmaking was "a disaster," but the second, in 1973, resulted in a quilt and started her on a career of teaching, lecturing, designing, and making quilts on commission. Paula's work has been widely exhibited, appeared in juried and invitational shows, and been featured in several quilt publications including *Lady's Circle Patchwork Quilts* and *Quilt.*

Despite the fact that all of Paula Lederkramer's designs are original, and her approach to the craft is contemporary in many ways, her outlook in one respect at least, is strictly traditional. She says, "I cannot bear to throw out a single piece of fabric, so I recycle everything. This fits in with my philosophy of quiltmaking as a salvage art. I am proud of my quilts since they do reflect this outlook."

Bonnie Leonard, born December 9, 1918, in Edgar County, Illinois, lives in Tangier, Indiana. She has been a quilter all her life, making her first quilt, a four-patch that she still has, at age six. Her numerous quilts since then, many for family members, have included a Maple Leaf for each of her two daughters, made from their childhood dresses. Bonnie, under the name of Mrs. Garnett Leonard, wrote "Grandma's Column" for the first seven issues of *Quilter's Newsletter Magazine,* and also contributed some of her original patterns.

She has this observation to make about a differentiation most quilters are aware of: "A good quilter does not necessarily mean a good seamstress. The best quilter among a Ladies' Aid Group never did a stitch of other sewing if she could help it."

Diana Leone, who is a native Californian, was born January 20, 1940, in Modesto, and lives in Santa Clara. Besides being a teacher, writer, designer, publisher, and owner of the shop Quilting Bee, Diana is also the maker of prize-winning quilts that have been featured in several publications including *The Great American Log Cabin Quilt Book* by Carol Anne Wien. She is the author of *The Sampler Quilt,* which has sold over 250,000 copies; *Investments; Fine Hand Quilting; Attic Windows: A Contemporary View;* and since 1982 has published the calendar *Quiltmakers.*

Diana Leone sees people as "the fibers of the fabric of life"; and about the learning process, be it in the field of quilting or elsewhere, she says, "The best students are forever students . . . there are no followers in the world of creative thinkers — just good listeners."

Linda Otto Lipsett, born June 9, 1947, in Dayton, Ohio, lives in Northridge, California. A violist, and studio musician for movies, television, and recordings, Linda started collecting antique quilts in the 1970's. The desire to know more about the people whose names were inscribed on the friendship quilts led to years of research and thousands of miles of travel , the results of which were, first an article, "A Piece of Ellen's Dress," appearing in *The Quilt Digest #2*, and then a book, *Remember Me: Women & Their Friendship Quilts*.

About future endeavors, Linda says, "My research of friendship quilts continues with many new adventures ahead, I am certain, for I never know where my quilts will lead me next."

Mildred Locke lives in the house in which she was born, October 10, 1919, on a farm in Bell Buckle, Tennessee. Since making her first quilt in 1960, Mildred has taught, lectured, judged, coordinated quilt shows, been the founding president of the Tennessee Valley Quilter's Association, and with her husband Edgar, owned and operated the shop Quilter's Haven from 1975 to 1987. She, the shop, and her quilt collection have been the subject of articles in several publications including *American Quilter* and *A People and Their Quilts* by John Rice Irwin. Her latest venture, undertaken with daughter Peggy Locke Bell, is designing appliqué quilt patterns.

Mildred offers this advice about living with quilts: "Don't keep them folded away. Quilts are like children . . . they need your love — take them out — show them off — enjoy them every day."

Diann Logan, born December 7, 1948, in Dallas, Texas, lives in Denver, Colorado. A classically trained musician who was lead vocalist and keyboardist for a Denver rock group, Diann taught herself to quilt in 1975. Of the over 90 quilts she has made since then, nearly all original designs, many have been widely exhibited, here and abroad, and featured in several publications including *Ms.* and *Quilter's Newsletter Magazine*. One of Diann's proudest accomplishments is "Freedom Wreath," her first appliqué piece. It represents 2,600 hours of work and was winner from Colorado and Judge's Choice in The Great American Quilt Contest, 1986. She is also the author of *Designs in Patchwork.*

Speaking of the article on her quilts in *Ms.* magazine, March 1983, she says, "[It] still thrills me — the quilts were included precisely because of their 'meaning' — the first time I felt I could talk to people through a visual art format."

Jessie MacDonald was born February 21, 1921, in Saskatoon, Saskatchewan, Canada. She died February 14, 1988. Although she learned to quilt when very young, and was fascinated by the patterns of the heavy quilts under which she slept as a child, she did not begin quilting in earnest until she had children of her own. Jessie taught quilting classes in New Jersey, where she had lived, and was active in the National Quilting Association, the North American Quilt Guild, and the New Jersey Quilting Teachers' Association. She was the co-author of *Let's Make a Patchwork Quilt,* and the author of *Let's Make More Patchwork Quilts.*

And to those students who anguished over every mistake, Jessie MacDonald would say, "A blind man on a galloping horse is never going to notice."

John Mangiapane lives in Waterbury, Connecticut, where he was born on May 12, 1955. A costume designer/maker who began making quilts in the late 1970s, John also teaches and writes. His work, both quilted and written, has appeared in numerous quilt magazines including *Quilt* and *Quilt World.* Among his proudest quilt accomplishments are winning the Best of Show Award at a local fair for seven years in a row, and selling his quilts "Kaleidoscope" and "Broken Star" into private collections.

Speaking of professionalism, John says, "A true professional in any area knows how to share. He respects the skills and talents of others and never overpowers others with demonstrations of his knowledge."

Gwen Marston, born in Sioux City, Iowa, and **Joe Cunningham,** born in Flint, Michigan, live on Beaver Island, Lake Michigan, in a home/studio they built themselves. Gwen and Joe, who began working together in 1979, first as musicians, then as quiltmakers, write, teach, lecture, exhibit widely, and have made over 100 quilts. Between them they have written articles for numerous publications, do a regular column for *Lady's Circle Patchwork Quilts,* are the authors of *Amish Quilting Patterns, 70 Classical Quilting Patterns, Sets and Borders, Q Is for Quilt,* and *American Beauties: Rose and Tulip Quilts,* and have produced five videos.

Serving as custodians for Mary Schafer's collection, they write, lecture, and arrange showings, and in 1980 Gwen published a catalogue of Mrs. Schafer's quilts with a commentary by Joe.

Of quilts, Gwen Marston says, "I never met a 9-patch quilt I didn't like."

And of quilts and art, Joe Cunningham observes, ". . . [they] are different. An artist who happens to make quilts cannot and should not be judged by the standards of quiltmaking. Quiltmakers, on the other hand, cannot and should not be judged by the standards of art."

Marsha McCloskey, born in Portland, Oregon, lives in Seattle, Washington. A quiltmaker, teacher, lecturer, and writer who began quilting in the 1970s, Marcia's work has appeared in several publications such as *Quilter's Newsletter Magazine* and *Pieces of the Past* by Nancy Martin. Some of her many books are *Small Quilts, Wall Quilts, Projects for Blocks and Borders, Christmas Quilts,* and *Feathered Star Quilts.*

Marsha McCloskey sees quilts as more than just bedcovers. "[They] speak to us of our collective and personal history — hardship, perseverance, caring, the good times and the bad, the work ethic, and creating beauty from scraps of fabric and bits of time."

Ione Benck McIntyre, born November 6, 1940, in Canby, Minnesota, graduated from Concordia College with a degree in education and music and lives in Bemidji, Minnesota. She began seriously quilting in 1966, when living in Alaska, and her involvement has since grown to include research, teaching, writing, and lecturing. In 1976, Ione was awarded a grant to tour southeast Alaska with a slide-lecture program and accompanying quiltmaking workshops on "American History in Patchwork." The program and workshops have also been presented throughout the United States. Her work has appeared in many quilt publications such as *Lady's Circle Patchwork Quilts*, and she is the author of *American History in Patchwork Patterns, Volume I: The Charter Oak*, the first of a series. Ione considers the research for these books, and pioneering the use of knits in making quilts to be her most important quilt-related accomplishments.

Of this last, she says, "It is my philosophy that any fabric used for clothing can be used successfully for beautiful quilts. When pioneer women began quilting, they used the materials at hand . . . . Today much of our clothing is polyester and cotton knits, so why not use them?"

Sally Medvidovich, born April 14, 1919, in Klana, Italy, came with her family at age two to join her father in Minnesota. Detained at Ellis Island for 40 days by the illness of a sister, Sally says, "We children loved the island. Three meals a day, clean sheets, and no war." She is another lifelong needleworker who did not come to quilting until adulthood, but since beginning in 1974 always has at least two quilts in process. Sally has also started exhibiting in her hometown of San Pedro, California, where she recently won her first ribbon. One of her own favorite quilts is "Lilies Medallion," which incorporates a black work embroidery center.

"My growing up years were during the depression," remembers Sally, "and there were good times and bad times. One quilt pattern is called 'Sunshine and Shadow,' and life is like that. My quilting helps get me through the bad times."

Dorothy Meisel, who as the daughter of a navy family lived in many different places during her childhood, was born October 9, 1918, in Belmar, New Jersey, and now makes her home in Rolling Hills Estates, California. A talented embroideress from her earliest years, Dorothy began quilting in 1974, and has since made numerous quilted gifts for family and friends, coordinated a Job's Daughters' quilt for a granddaughter, and, for herself, worked a full-size Hawaiian quilt. Her proudest accomplishment has been the designing, coordinating, and bringing to completion the 1976 Bicentennial Quilt of the Auxiliary to the American Optometric Association. This 9¼′ x 11¾′ quilt has blocks from auxiliaries in all 50 states, plus one from each of the nation's ten optometric schools, and a special block designed by Dr. Harry Meisel honoring Benjamin Franklin. After being the star of several shows, it is on permanent display at the American Optometric Association headquarters and museum in St. Louis, Missouri.

Of quilting, Dorothy says, "It has opened wide the doors and windows to the best times of my life."

Suellen Jackson Meyer, born April 12, 1944, in Rutherford, Tennessee, "a town of 1,000 people, 500 of whom were quilters," lives in Creve Coeur, Missouri. An associate professor of English at St. Louis Community College, she is a writer, lecturer, quilt historian, and collector whose work has appeared in several publications including *The Quilt Digest #4*, ("Pine Tree Quilts"). Suellen feels her most important quilt accomplishments are her research, which looks at quilts from a regional perspective, and collecting Missouri quilts before other collectors thought they mattered. This collection has over 130 Missouri and Illinois quilts, and reveals "the mid-American quiltmaker to be as creative, talented, and skilled as any . . . ."

Suellen Meyer, speaking of her research, sees as one of its main goals "an attempt to put quilts back into the history of women so that we see the cultural imperatives and emotional content which led to specific types of quilts."

Elaine T. Miles, born December 24, 1932, in Boston, Massachusetts, graduated from Girls' Latin School and Boston State Teacher's College, and lives in San Pedro, California. She began quilting in 1972, taught for several years, lectured sporadically, and since 1979 has been half of the publishing company, R. & E. Miles. Quilt accomplishments include the books *Quilts and Quotes: A Birthday Book, Many Hands: Making a Communal Quilt,* and *Patchwork Year: A Datebook,* and having a quilt on the cover of *Harper's* magazine.

Speaking of her twin passions, quilts and books, Elaine says, "I feel they are related in many ways, not the least of which is, I see them both, *real* books and *real* quilts — those that ask something of us — as an endangered species."

Margaret J. Miller, born February 7, 1946, in Wenatchee, Washington, has degrees in textiles and clothing from the University of Maryland and the University of Wisconsin, and lives in San Marcos, California. A needleworker since childhood, and quilter since the 1970s, Margaret's first "public works" were a series of banners for her sons' soccer teams. She began to consider herself a serious quiltmaker in 1981, and teaches, lectures, and makes quilts that have been widely exhibited, appeared in many publications such as *Quilter's Newsletter Magazine,* and been purchased for walls of homes, businesses, and hospitals. Among her own favorite quilting accomplishments are serving as Artist-in-Residence at the 1986 Asilomar Conference and producing small wall hangings for folk art shops nationwide, including the Smithsonian Museum Shops in Washington, D.C.

Speaking of her work, Margaret Miller says, "I feel that everything I've done has been an apprenticeship to the next thing."

Theresa Millett, born July 14, 1935, in Readfield, Maine, grew up in North Jay, Maine, and lives in Connecticut. Although she has loved needlework all her life and made a few "very poor" quilts early on, it was not until the 1970s that she learned to quilt "properly." Theresa still considers herself more of an "appreciator" than accomplished quilter and is working on an ongoing "Lexicon Series," made up of small nap-size quilts representing the different types of quilts.

Theresa thinks all quilts, "from the simplest and most traditional to contemporary fiber art, must have three things to succeed: color, proportion, and soul."

Virginia Jean Cox Mitchell, a native Kansan who lives in Lawrence, was born July 30, 1931, in Kingman, where her parents were wheat farmers, and studied home economics and design at the University of Kansas. She learned to sew as a child, and in making her first quilt in 1964, a Log Cabin, remembered her grandmother basting hexagons over pieces of paper, and has used this English method of piecing in all her work since. Many of Jean's designs, such as "Wheat Centennial," "Heart of the Nation," and a fanciful cloak of childhood memories, "Kansas Windmill," have been inspired by Kansas. Her work has appeared in several publications including *Lady's Circle Patchwork Quilts, Quilter's Newsletter Magazine*, and *The Quilt Engagement Calendar 1986;* and she is the author of *Quilt Kansas!*, a collection of patterns and commentary, the proceeds of which go to the care of the quilt collection in the Spencer Museum of Art, University of Kansas, Lawrence.

Jean used to give programs, but now uses the time for quilting. On this setting of priorities and following through, she says, "It's a lot easier to get in over your head than it is to get out again."

Mildred L. Morgon, born June 10, 1920, in Holtville, California, to which her father, a cotton farmer, and her mother, an accomplished seamstress, migrated from Texas in 1910, lives in Long Beach, California. She graduated from Central Jr. College (her mother in those depression days bartering two quilts a month to pay for Mildred's and her sister's room and board) and St. Francis School of Nursing, San Francisco. In 1974, she and a daughter-in-law opened The Hearth, a quilting and gift shop, which also sponsored an annual quilt show.

Mildred's philosophy of life, broadly paraphrased, is: "I'll pass this way just once, so enjoy!"

Patricia J. Morris, born December 27, 1934, in Aurora, Illinois, lives in Glassboro, New Jersey. A teacher, lecturer, judge, and writer whose serious involvement with quilting began in 1975, Pat's articles and columns have been appearing regularly in several publications since 1976. She is a contributing editor for *American Quilter* and *Quilt World* magazines, her series "Judging Prize-winning Quilts" for the latter having been reprinted as a booklet, and from 1972 to 1976 she also offered a correspondence course in quilting.

For those who think judging a quilt show is just a matter of picking out the quilt you like best, Patricia Morris says, "Judging a quilt competition provides a special challenge. It requires total concentration, the ability to think on your feet, to make decisions and, above all, maintain objectivity."

Caron L. Mosey of Flushing, Michigan, was born February 25, 1956, in Flint, Michigan, and studied at C.S. Mott Community College, Olivet College, and the University of Michigan, and was a vocal scholarship winner at Interlochen Fine Arts Camp. A quiltmaker, teacher, and lecturer, Caron is a contributing editor for *Quilt* magazine, writes regularly for several other publications, and is the author of *America's Pictorial Quilts* and *Contemporary Quilts from Traditional Designs*. Her quilts, too, have appeared in many magazines such as *Quilt World*, and been widely exhibited. She considers her two books, and the quilts "Jack's Beanstalk" (an original design) and "Ocean Waves," to be among her most important quilting accomplishments.

Caron worries lest quiltmakers lose sight of the main

reason for making quilts, and says, "So many quiltmakers make quilts with the sole purpose of pleasing a judge or of grabbing the public's attention that they forget the best part of quiltmaking — the *fun* of it."

Kathy Munkelwitz, born August 2, 1940, in Minneapolis, Minnesota, lives on a 160-acre farm just outside Isle, Minnesota, where she and her husband raise sheep. Besides tending a 100-ewe flock — which means spending most of April in the barn — Kathy is a full-time quilter, designer, lecturer, teacher, and writer who sells custom-made quilts from her home as well as original patterns by mail. Her work has appeared in several quilt publications including *Quilt* and *Stitch 'n Sew Quilts,* and she is the author of *The I've Never Made a Quilt Before Quilt Book.*

And about those stepchildren of quiltdom, Kathy Munkelwitz says, "I always get a bit irritated with myself and others when we refer to a quilt as 'just a tied quilt.' Tied or tufted quilts are the basic form of quilts, made mainly from scraps, quickly put together to use immediately. They are the useable, drag-around, everyday wrap-ups we all love."

Anita Murphy of Kountze, Texas, was born May 15, 1927, in Kansas City, Kansas, and grew up in Omaha, Nebraska, and Tulsa, Oklahoma. A teacher, lecturer, judge, and writer, Anita's earliest quilt, made at age seven for her doll, won a first prize. Some years later, another prize-winner, "Freedom to Dream," winner from the state of Texas in The Great American Quilt Contest, 1986, is one of her proudest quilt accomplishments. Her other achievements include volunteer teaching at the Center for Older Adults, founding The Golden Triangle Quilt Guild, and being one of nine founding members of The Texas Heritage Quilt Society. This last was responsible for documenting over 1,900 quilts and producing the book *Texas Quilts, Texas Treasures,* the proceeds from which go toward a Texas quilt museum. Anita's work has also appeared in several quilt publications including *Quilt* magazine.

Anita Murphy's own private Golden Rule says, ". . . life

in general, and quilting in particular, is more fun when we show our love and care for each other."

Paula Nadelstern lives in New York City where she was born on May 8, 1951. An occupational therapist whose quiltmaking career began with making baby quilts, first for friends, then for her own daughter, she has designed, coordinated, and brought to completion over a dozen group quilts. Paula loves the camaraderie of people working together in such an effort, and it was from this interest that her book *Quilting Together*, written with LynNell Hancock, grew. Her own quilts have been featured in several publications including *America's Pictorial Quilts* by Caron L. Mosey and *America's Glorious Quilts* by Dennis Duke and Deborah Harding; and "Reflections on Grandma's Wall" was the winner from the State of New York in The Great American Quilt Contest, 1986. Personal favorites include "Fairy Tales" and "Kady's Butterflies."

Of the work of quilting, Paula Nadelstern says, "[It] tends to be an isolated experience, which I relish as I obsess over color, shape and detail. But it is important to remember the context in which our quilts are made and viewed: a world in which we make connections and take responsibilities."

Julia Overton Needham lives in Knoxville, Tennessee, where she was born on December 21, 1924. Julia's first quilt, "A Trip Around the World," started in 1941, was finished in 1976 when she began seriously quilting. Since then she has made over 15 quilts which together have won more than 58 awards and been widely exhibited. Her work has appeared in numerous publications including the *Quilt Art '85 Engagement Calendar*, *Quilt Art '88 Engagement Calendar*, and *A People and Their Quilts* by John Rice Irwin. In 1986, she was received into the Master Quilters' Guild for her masterpiece quilt, "Wintergreen," a rare honor, and her proudest quilting achievement.

"I'm a dedicated quilter," says Julia. "It gives me a good feeling of accomplishment. I can just lose myself and shut the world out."

Cyril I. Nelson, born May 6, 1927, in Baltimore, Maryland, lives in New York City. An editor at E.P. Dutton, Nelson's name has become synonymous in the minds of most quilters with *The Quilt Engagement Calendar*, which he has compiled annually since 1975. In 1982, 185 quilts were gleaned from eight years worth of calendars to produce *The Quilt Engagement Calendar Treasury*, co-authored with Carter Houck. Of his quilt-related accomplishments, he regards the publication of *America's Quilts and Coverlets* by Carleton L. Safford and Robert Bishop (1972), and *A Gallery of Amish Quilts* by Robert Bishop and Elizabeth Safanda (1976), as his most important.

And for those quilters who worry lest some year there might not be enough quilts to fill a new engagement calendar, Cyril I. Nelson says, "One of the several joys of working and studying American quilts is knowing that no matter how many beautiful examples have already been recorded there are still more waiting to be discovered."

Charlotte Patera of Novato, California, was born 1927 in Detroit, Michigan, and grew up in Ohio. An art major in college, she studied two years at a commercial art school, and worked 15 years in the graphic design field before teaching herself to quilt in the early 1970s. Charlotte is a teacher, lecturer, and writer best known for her work in reverse appliqué and mola making. One of the highlights of her creative life was "to visit the Kuna Indians on the San Blas Islands, live among them for a few days, stitch with them, and eventually discover how molas are really made . . . ." Her articles, designs, and quilts have been featured in many publications such as *Quilter's Newsletter Magazine*, and her books include *The Appliqué Book*, *The Mola Pattern Book*, *The Stained Glass Pattern Book for Reverse Appliqué*, *Cutwork Appliqué*, and *Mola Making*.

Speaking of needlework, Charlotte Patera says, "Spending long hours to create something beautiful helps to slow down the world a bit. It also produces something that gives us back our individuality and assures us that our identity will not be lost forever in the form of a computerized number."

Linda Marusarz Platt lives in Chicago, Illinois, where she was born November 8, 1948. A seamstress and jewelry maker until she saw her first quilt in 1972, Linda says of that experience, ". . . a friend gave me a quilt that his grandmother had made. I was amazed that anyone could possibly cut all those tiny pieces and do all those hours of sewing! You'd have to be crazy or have nothing else to do, I thought. Since then I have made about 45 quilts, and also married the friend who first showed me one." Some of those 45 quilts have been featured in *Quilter's Newsletter Magazine* and include a Crazy quilt with original embroidery designs, "Some Bears Over the Rainbow," and "The Polish Quilt," a tribute to her origins.

Linda feels her most important quilting accomplishment has been to teach children to quilt, and says of it, "the best thing I ever learned, and the best thing I ever taught."

Doris Amiss Rabey, born in Washington, D.C., has spent all her life in the area, making her home in nearby Hyattsville, Maryland. She learned to quilt in 1973 in order to finish two inherited tops, and has since made many prize-winning quilts. Although she finds it difficult to choose a favorite, Doris is particularly fond of "Feathered Star," featured in the *Quilt Art '86 Engagement Calendar*, the "President's Wreath Variation," purchased by the American Quilter's Society for their museum, and "Whirligig," for which her husband, Jim, did all the cutting. Her work has also appeared in several other quilt publications including *American Quilter* and *Quilter's Newsletter Magazine.*

Speaking of quilting, Doris says, ". . . can't you just feel the pride in being able to make a quilt? We know everyone can't."

Lahoma Butler Rackley lives in Carnegie, Oklahoma, where she was born July 13, 1914. Graduating from what was then called Oklahoma College for Women, she taught business courses at Carnegie Jr. College and the local high school until her marriage. Lahoma began to quilt almost as soon as she could hold a needle, and the over 50 quilts she has made in her lifetime are part of a family collection covering six generations of quiltmakers. This collection has been widely exhibited and is also the subject of Lahoma's slide shows and talks. Other quilt achievements include helping found the Central Oklahoma Quilters' Guild, the column "Letters from Lahoma," a regular feature of *Stitch 'n Sew Quilts* since 1983, and the book, *The Quiet Comfort of Quilts — Stitches of Love from Lahoma*, stories of her 70 years as a quilter.

Lahoma's philosophy is, "Try to accomplish something worthwhile each day. If not pleased, make up for it the next day."

Bets Ramsey lives in Chattanooga, Tennessee, where she was born June 9, 1923. A writer, researcher, quiltmaker, and authority on Southern quilts, she became interested in quilts when doing a research paper for graduate work at the University of Tennessee in 1971. Bets has been the director of The Southern Quilt Symposium since 1973 and written the column "The Quilter" for *The Chattanooga Times* since 1981. Her work has appeared in other publications such as *Quilter's Newsletter Magazine* as well, and she is the co-author of *The Quilts of Tennessee: Images of Domestic Life Prior to 1930*, and author of *Quilt Close-up: Five Southern Views* and *Old and New Quilt Patterns in the Southern Tradition.*

Bets Ramsey is also an exhibiting artist in textiles with more than 60 one-woman shows to her credit. She says, "There is no such thing as a bad color. It is how you use it that matters."

Judy Rehmel, lives in Richmond, Indiana, and although born April 29, 1936, in Bay County, Michigan, considers herself a Hoosier because most of her life has been spent in Indiana. A media director for an advertising agency, Judy, in 1978, feeling the need for a pattern identification book, published the first of her *Keys to 1000 Quilting Patterns*. Three other *Keys* followed, and in 1986 all four books were brought together by Prentice Hall and published as *The Pattern I.D. Book*. Another book, *Key to 1000 Appliqué Quilt Patterns*, was published in 1984.

Of contemporary quilting, Judy says, "We no longer quilt because we have to: we quilt because we want to — a way of expressing true beauty."

Penny Rigdon lives in Washington, D.C., where she was born. A graduate of Barnard College, Penny was one of the seven founders and first president (1970) of the National Quilting Association. She has spent her life immersed in quilts, quilt designs, and quilt people, and believes that doing and studying one real quilt can teach more than any number of books, pictures, and slides. Her accomplishments include teaching "many people to quilt to the best quality standards they can achieve," and arranging for volunteers to work on quilt tops both at the Renwick Gallery of the Smithsonian during the showing of the Jonathan Holstein-Gail Van der Hoof collection in 1972, and during the six-week run of the play *Quilters* at Kennedy Center in 1984.

Penny Rigdon is especially proud of a piece titled, "About Quilts," written for the July 1973 issue of *embroiderer's journal*. In this article she says, ". . . the best source of knowledge about quilts is quilts, but . . . the everyday quilt quite simply perished, used up in daily living." The final sentences tell us, ". . . what we must come to do is appreciate the great history of quilts for what it is, the chronicle of hearth and home, something that will never truly be written down, but passed from parent to child in a private way.

"The important thing to carry on is serious craftsmanship, striving for excellence and beauty. We must forgo accuracy of lost facts and settle for accuracy in cutting and sewing. We can do new things today, and make up new names if we wish, and still be working in the fine tradition of our great grandmothers."

Vivian Ritter of Evergreen, Colorado, was born December 25, 1945, in Stillwater, Oklahoma, and lived for several years in New Hampshire. As co-owner of a children's shop, The Red Balloon, she began quilting, and designing clothes and toys, but serious involvement came with the discovery of Seminole patchwork and strip-piecing. Vivian's work has appeared in such publications as *Stitch 'n Sew Quilts* as well as *Quilter's Newsletter Magazine*, on whose staff she's been since 1983. Other quilt accomplishments include writing, teaching, lecturing, putting together a series of slide shows on quilt art for the New England Quilters' Guild, and a book, *Patchwork Potpourri*, a collection of original designs.

Vivian's approach to quilting is a love of the doing. "I should have been a draftsman as I love everything about the process."

Judy Robbins, a native of Connecticut, was born March 8, 1945, in Danbury, and lives in Glastonbury. Judy, who makes contemporary wall quilts and clothing and has been a writer, lecturer, and teacher in the field of quilts, works in business communications, editing *Shuttle, Spindle & Dyepot,* quarterly magazine of the Handweavers' Guild. Co-author of *Not Just Another Quilt* and *Hands All Around: Making Cooperative Quilts*, her work has also appeared in publications such as *Lady's Circle Patchwork Quilts* and *Quilt.*

In the text accompanying The Ribbon segment she made honoring Chief Joseph, the Nez Perce Indian chief, Judy Robbins said, "After Chief Joseph had exhausted every possible means to achieve a large-scale peace and failed, he vowed at least to maintain his commitment to peace on a personal level. If many of us were to do the same, I believe that a profound shift in consciousness would occur."

Art Salemme of Riverdale, Maryland, was born in Boston, Massachusetts, in 1923, but has lived in the Washington, D.C., area most of his life. Art has always been interested in the needlearts, and says, "Since my retirement in 1979, I've been able to devote 120% of my time to them." A coeditor and editor for many years of *Patchwork Patter*, quarterly journal of the National Quilting Association, his work has also appeared in several quilt publications including *America's Pictorial Quilts* by Caron L. Mosey. He is the author of *A Patchwork House Christmas, A Quilter's Bouquet, A Garden of Roses*, and an *NQA Sampler of Quilt Baskets*.

Art's advice to those who might be intimidated by the conflicting opinions of what constitutes a proper quilt is, "If you want to make a quilt with an unusual nontraditional color scheme, or otherwise break with quilting tradition, do so boldly, because that's you! Conversely, if you're the kind of person who delights in reproducing a quilt with historically correct fabrics and workmanship, then do that boldly too, with no trepidation. Because 'you are what you are.' . . ."

Marina Ratliff Salume, born August 1, 1951, in Chicago, Illinois, lives in Daly City, California. Marina, who works in advertising, has a degree in fashion and graphic design from the Minneapolis College of Art and Design. Since she began quilting in 1979, her work has been widely exhibited, received numerous awards, and been featured in a one-woman show at the American Museum of Quilts and Related Arts, San Jose, California (1985). She believes her best-known quilt is "Kimono Memory." Made to commemorate a trip to Japan, it has won prizes, appeared in both Japanese and American quilt magazines, and is the subject of a poster. Marina has also been a frequent contributor to *Quilt World* and *Quilt World Omnibook*.

Speaking of priorities, she says, "Quilting is very important to me, but the people I love come first. There are quilts I never made because people needed me, and that's as it should be. On the other hand, when I'm alone, quilts console me. I can always depend on them, whereas people are not so dependable. A well-balanced life needs both. The trick is trying to keep them in balance."

Mary Schafer of Flushing, Michigan, was born in 1910 in Austria, coming to the United States when she was four. A needleworker since childhood, Mary began seriously quilting in 1956, and as part of her quilt education read extensively, corresponded with other quilters, and started collecting old quilts in order to study them. Her collection, those quilts she has acquired and those she has made, numbers over 200 and has appeared in numerous publications such as *Lady's Circle Patchwork Quilts* and *Quilters' Journal* and been the subject of many exhibitions and a catalogue, *The Mary Schafer Quilt Collection* by Gwen Marston. On September 12, 1986, the state of Michigan, in Resolution Number 605, declared Mary Schafer "one of Michigan's most prominent quiltmakers and historians."

Speaking of one of quiltmaking's fringe benefits, Mary says, "Today, the world lives so fast people don't have any time to think. Any type of quiltmaking takes time, but gives time to think and work with one's hands."

Joyce Schlotzhauer of Painted Post, New York, was born in Bluffton, Indiana, and lived for a while in São Paulo, Brazil. A teacher, writer, lecturer, and designer who taught herself to quilt, Joyce's "maiden" quilt won first prize in a national exhibition (1974). Other quilt accomplishments include designing and supervising (from Brazil) the construction of the Corning (New York) Quilters' Guild Bicentennial Sampler Quilt, a widely exhibited prize-winner; doing a piece for the Corning Public Library; and serving as quilter-in-residence for the Southern Tier Library System of New York. Her work has appeared in several quilt magazines such as *Lady's Circle Patchwork Quilts*, and she is the author of *The Curved Two-Patch System, Curves Unlimited*, and *Cutting Up with the Curved Two-Patch.*

Joyce feels her most important quilting achievement has been the development of the curved two-patch system which produced not only a new piecing and design technique, but the awareness that "learning in depth gives students special insights . . . . The discipline of in-depth study, in whatever segment of quilting, is something I wish every quilter will ultimately try after having a short fill of workshops which can only touch the surface of new ideas."

Joan Schulze, born October 13, 1936, in Chicago, Illinois, lives in Sunnyvale, California. After "careers of teaching in the public schools and being a wife and mother of four," Joan feels fortunate to have found in quilting what she wants to do with the rest of her life. A quilter, artist, teacher, and lecturer, she has exhibited widely, both in one-woman shows such as "Quilt Poems and Dreams" at the Villa Montalvo Center for the Arts, Saratoga, California, and as part of group exhibitions including "Five Artists: Quilts," San Francisco Art Gallery, and "The Art Quilt," a traveling show sponsored by the Art Museum Association of America. Her work has appeared in numerous publications among which have been *The Quilt Digest #3*, and *The Art Quilt* by Penny McMorris and Michael Kile.

Joan loves making quilts, thinking about them, and seeing how they affect others, and says "The remarkable thing is that everything I have learned beforehand has been necessary in what I do now. It makes one move closer to believing in a grand plan."

Doris Scott, born December 4, 1934, in Chicago, Illinois, lives in San Pedro, California. Doris, who has been a needleperson all her life, began quilting in 1975. She has taught, exhibited, designed, and coordinated many group quilts, and likes to incorporate quilt techniques into wearable art.

Although quilting has top priority, her interest extends to other fiberarts and she has been studying loom weaving.

Family and job responsibilities are not allowing Doris Scott all the time she'd like for her quilting, but she knows it's "a true love that will never die — I'll get back to it."

Helen R. Scott lives in Portsmouth, Ohio, where she was born August 24, 1925. A painter in oils and pastels, Helen's first quilt was made in 1959 to match a painting. There have been over 50 quilts since, the earliest ones designed for her three children. Her quilts and blocks have been featured in many issues of *Quilt World Omnibook*, and won more than 30 prizes. "Cat Quilt," chosen by UNICEF to appear on notes and postcards, is one of Helen's proudest achievements, "knowing that the sales from it has helped needy children is so rewarding to me." She also teaches both quilting and painting.

Speaking of inspiration she says, "The shape of a flower, petal, or leaf, or the color of a piece of fabric can give me an idea for a whole quilt . . . or two."

Eleanor Hamilton Sienkiewicz of Washington, D.C., was born January 6, 1942, in Mineola, New York, and grew up in a suburb of Princeton, New Jersey. Elly, who was making her own clothes in fifth grade, and has a degree in history from Wellesley College, began teaching quilting in the early 1970s. A writer, designer, researcher, and publisher, her work has appeared in many quilt publications including the *Quilt Art '87 Engagement Calendar* and *Quilter's Newsletter Magazine*. Among her proudest quilt accomplishments are the co-founding of Cabin Fever Calicoes (1978), a mail order quilt supply business, and research on Baltimore Album quilts, which resulted in the book *Spoken Without a Word*. She is also the author of *Baltimore Beauties and Beyond: A Workbook in Classic Appliqué*.

Of writing her books midst schedules that included teaching, lecturing, and family responsibilities, Elly says, "[It] was a respite with the things I cherish most: sense of family and one's bounty, the human saga and history, beauty and the communion of quiltmaking."

Ami Simms, born November 12, 1954, in Detroit, Michigan, lives in Flint, Michigan. Ami began quilting in 1976 when, as part of her research for a thesis, she stayed with an Amish family and was introduced to the craft. A quiltmaker, lecturer, teacher, and writer whose quilts have been widely exhibited, she is a contributing editor for *Quilt* magazine, and writes frequently for other magazines as well. Among the many publications in which Ami's quilts have been featured are the *Quilt Art '85 Engagement Calendar* and *America's Pictorial Quilts* by Caron L. Mosey. She is the author of *Little Ditties, Appliqué,* and *How to Improve Your Quilting Stitch.*

As for choosing which quilt to make, Ami Simms has this advice: ". . . take a stand and decide to make only quilts that please you . . . . Listen to the advice of shopowners, workshop leaders, authors, and other assorted experts, but in the end remember that you're going to live with the quilt, so go with your heart and be your own expert."

Fran Soika, a native of Ohio, was born January 17, 1924, in Cleveland and lives in Novelty. She made her first quilt in 1956, but it was not until 1968 that quilting became, after the needs of her family, top priority. Her work since then has been exhibited widely, received many awards, and been featured in numerous publications including *The Quilt Engagement Calendar* for 1982, 1983, 1985, and 1986. Although the making of each quilt is important to Fran, she numbers among her proudest achievements winning Best of Show in the Russell Art Show, four years out of eight; being accepted in the Cleveland Museum of Art "May Show," four times (winning the $1,000 Craft Award in 1982); and having the quilt "Polynesia, the Sky" chosen as cover for *The Quilt Engagement Calendar 1983.*

Of the work yet undone, Fran Soika says, "I cannot wait until I get up in the morning to get started. I will probably go to that Great Quilt World in the Sky with a needle, thread, and thimble, and my first unfinished project."

Willow Ann Soltow, born December 29, 1955, in Attleboro, Massachusetts, graduated from Brown University, and lives in Clinton, Connecticut. Willow, who is an editor for the Humane Society of the United States, began quilting at 15, and her work has appeared in several quilt magazines including *Quilt* and *Quilt World*. She is also the author of the *Kid's Very Own Quilt Book*, and *Making Animal Quilts*.

Willow feels that "one of the most exciting things about quilts is the way they reveal important themes in quilters' lives. For me, one of these themes is animals — or animal protection — I strongly believe that teaching people — especially children — to be compassionate toward animals is a step toward creating a more caring world."

Elaine Sparlin of Lenexa, Kansas, was born February 18, 1915, in Missouri. Elaine, who began quilting at 12, started making story quilts in 1976 after working on a quilt for Edward Larson. Since then, her quilts have won awards, been widely exhibited, and featured in numerous publications including *America's Pictorial Quilts* by Caron L. Mosey. Among her proudest achievements are "Not by Bread Alone," which traveled with an exhibition of antique and contemporary quilts sponsored by the Association of Community Arts Council of Kansas, 1978; "The Good Old Days," cover quilt for *Quilt*, Spring, 1981; and "The Quilting Bee," Blue Ribbon winner from the National Quilt Association and cover quilt for the *Quilt Art '85 Engagement Calendar*.

Speaking of words to live by, Elaine Sparlin says, "I grew up with a number of quotes which I should have learned to disregard years ago . . . [one is] 'Idle hands are the devil's workshop.' It is all right to have quiet times for reflection, relaxation, and planning the next quilt design."

Jeannie M. Spears, born June 4, 1934, in Sault Ste. Marie, Michigan, lives in Vadnais Heights, Minnesota. A quiltmaker, teacher, lecturer, writer, and judge whose hand-dyed, hand-quilted quilts have received national recognition, Jeannie's quilting career began in the early 1970s. Other accomplishments include the books *Teaching Basic Quiltmaking* (editor), *Confidence Quilting Home Study Course,* and *Mastering the Basics of Quiltmaking;* serving on the National Quilting Association's board as chairman of both the Teacher Certification Program and Master Quilter's Guild Program; and editing and publishing *The Professional Quilter*, a magazine she started in 1983. Her work has also appeared in several quilt publications, among which have been *Lady's Circle Patchwork Quilts* and the *Quiltmakers 1987* calendar.

Of seemingly unpromising beginnings, Jeannie says, "Today's hobbyist may become tomorrow's craftsperson."

Milly Splitstone, a native of Michigan, was born April 29, 1926, in rural Newaygo and lives in nearby Fremont. Milly, who helped tie family quilts as a high schooler and made her first quilt, "A Sunbonnet Girl," in 1939, returned to serious quilting in 1979 after a 25-year absence. A quiltmaker, teacher, researcher, judge, and organizer of quilt shows, her proudest quilt accomplishments include the book *Michigan Quilters and Their Designs* (co-author), and the quilt "Michigan Winter," made for its cover.

And in an original verse, "Value of Prayer," Milly Splitstone writes:

> "The gold drops in my garden
> Bow their heads to the ground
> Thanking God for the drink of fresh rain."

Odette Goodman Teel, born December 15, 1927, in Chicago, Illinois, lives in Long Beach, California. An embroideress, maker of banners, and needlework teacher, Odette became interested in quilting after working on a number of group projects. Her quilt accomplishments since then have included a series of slide lectures on group quilts, a memory quilt for son Harry, and her own group quilts, "Ms. Sue: Alive and Liberated," and "Sunbonnet Sue as the Subject of Favorite Paintings." Of these last, "Ms. Sue," has been widely exhibited and featured in such publications as *Quilter's Newsletter Magazine,* and *America's Glorious Quilts* by Dennis Duke and Deborah Harding.

For additional words to live and stitch by, Odette has embroidered and hung on her workroom wall this original motto: "Simple Is Best."

Judy Schroeder Tomlonson, born May 27, 1939, at Newton, Kansas, was raised in the Tabor Church (General Conference Mennonite) near Goessel, Kansas, and lives in Warrensburg, Missouri, where her husband is a pastor to a Church of Brethren congregation. Judy, whose love of quilts has been enriched by the influence of her grandmother, teaching of her mother, and a background in art, teaches basic quilting techniques, conducts workshops on Mennonite and Amish quilts, sells wallhangings to a Washington, D.C., shop, and is the author of *Mennonite Quilts and Pieces.* In 1987, she was awarded a grant from the National Quilting Association to document pre-1940 Amish and Mennonite quilts in 15 states and three Canadian provinces.

Speaking of a quilt's special qualities, Judy Tomlonson says, "A quilt is not just a quilt. It is not an inanimate object only to be spread on a bed or hung on a wall. It is the repository of special memories . . . it is a time recalled . . . ."

Nan Tournier, who was born May 19, 1945, in Hinsdale, Illinois, has lived in Charleston, South Carolina, for so many years she considers herself "southern." She taught herself to quilt when her mother bought 12 blocks at a garage sale, and has since made over 30 full-sized quilts and introduced hundreds of other women (her mother among them) to the joys of quilting. Nan's quilts have been widely exhibited, won numerous prizes, and been featured in several quilting publications including the *Quilt Art '87 Engagement Calendar* and *First Prize Quilts* by Dimetra Makris.

Regarding the pursuit of perfection, Nan offers this advice concerning quilts: "Don't be afraid to make mistakes, fabric is very forgiving." Speaking of life in general, she says, ". . . concentrate on doing your best wherever you are at the moment rather than worrying about, or seeking, future glory."

Louise Owens Townsend, born February 14, 1942, in Washington, D.C., lives in Denver, Colorado. A retired Spanish teacher and history researcher, Louise's interest in quilts began with a "Star of Bethlehem" that was a wedding present. Her earliest quilting was done on group quilts, including a Douglas County (Kansas) Bicentennial quilt she helped organize. The first quilt made on her own was a sampler, winner of four blue ribbons. Managing editor of *Quilter's Newsletter Magazine*, Louise has been with Leman Publications since 1978, and readers over the years have benefited from her knowledge of, and wide-ranging interest in, all phases of quilting. She collects antique and contemporary quilts, and makes two or three small quilts a year.

When going through her quotations, she said it was interesting to observe "both the changes in subject matter, . . . and the ideas that seemed to repeat over and over" which could well be a comment on the journey through life.

Betty Mae Simpson Treasure, born January 12, 1924, in Erie, Colorado, lives in Tucson, Arizona, in a house she and her husband built themselves. A self-taught quilter who started piecing quilts to use up scraps, Betty began making theme quilts after she worked out a personal method of doing appliqué. Her quilts include: "The Hobbit" (inspired by J.R.R. Tolkein's book), "Desert Photo Fun" (birds and animals), "The Dancers," "American First Family" (Navajo life), and "Southwestern Heritage" (a commission for a woman in Switzerland). All these carefully researched quilts have taken many prizes and been featured in *Quilt World Omnibook.* A later work, using the black-and-white pottery designs of the Mimbres Indians, is for a museum in Piños Altos, New Mexico.

When she finished "Southwestern Heritage," Betty wrote the following verse:

"I have arms that are numb and mincemeat fingers,
Just finished a quilt and the pain still lingers,
But give me a week or so to recover
And I'll be ready to quilt another!"

Susan K. Turbak of Cambridge, Massachusetts, was born April 24, 1950, in Schenectady, New York. Susan's quilting career began in a dulcimer class where she met Nancy Halpern, who persuaded her to learn to quilt. A dulcimer case, her first project, was finished in 1978, followed by a full-size quilt in 1979. Susan has since gone on to explore the use of free-form appliqué in landscape quilts, and her work has been widely exhibited and featured in several publications including *America's Pictorial Quilts* by Caron L. Mosey and *Quilter's Newsletter Magazine.* Among her other quilt accomplishments are teaching, designing a small silk flag launched on the shuttle Challenger, July 29, 1985 (the first "quilt" in space), and being involved with a studio quilt program for the Newton (Massachusetts) Arts in the Park.

Susan Turbak believes that ". . . whether the quilts are antique, scrap, or contemporary designs, there is a place for all in the world, and they look wonderful together."

Emily Jane Walden was born December 10, 1930, in the county of Hampshire, England, moving in 1937 to northwestern Massachusetts where she still lives. Practicing a life-style of voluntary simplicity for most of her adult life, Emily keeps a journal of lessons learned that she hopes might someday serve as a guide for others wanting to live more simply without "becoming eccentric or estranged from the larger world." Her convictions extend to needlework, and in the past 15 years she has made over a dozen quilts for which nothing was purchased except thread and an occasional batt.

Speaking of quilting in the late 20th century, Emily says, "In spite of all the talk of giving us time and an appreciation of simpler things, I worry that quilting is in danger of becoming just another part of the problem of frantic consumption and activity, instead of one of the solutions as it should be."

Sydne Marie Yanko-Jongbloed lives in San Pedro, California, where she was born May 18, 1952. She studied at California State University, Long Beach, receiving a degree in French and doing graduate work in educational psychology. Sydne began quilting in 1980, opening her shop, Quilt Sails, the following year. Among her quilt accomplishments are teaching, making (with her mother) Freedom quilts for nine nieces and nephews, and coordinating many group quilts for community projects. The latter have included "Windows on the Sea" for the Cabrillo Marine Museum, San Pedro, and two quilts to raise funds for battered women.

Sydne, who as the mother of four young boys, often doesn't have all the quilting time she'd like, says, "My children are the only creative projects I have been able to take on and finish in the prescribed time of nine months."

The Authors

Adams, Henry [Brooks]. 1838-1918. American historian and scholar. Author of *The Education of Henry Adams* (1906).

Addison, Joseph. 1672-1719. English poet, critic, statesman, and writer. Best known for his *Spectator* essays (1711-1714).

Agathon. Late fifth century B.C. Athenian tragic poet. Friend of Euripides and Plato.

Ahbez, Eden. 1908- . American composer and author.

Alcott, Amos Bronson. 1799-1888. American transcendentalist, teacher, and writer.

Allen, Frederick Lewis. 1890-1954. American editor and writer.

Allen, Woody. 1935- . American film director, writer, and actor.

Allingham, William. 1824-1889. Irish poet and editor.

Alma-Tadema, Laurence. 1865-1940. English poet and writer. Daughter and namesake of pre-Raphaelite painter Sir Lawrence Alma-Tadema.

Amiel, Henri Frédéric. 1821-1881. Swiss poet and philosopher.

Aquinas, St. Thomas. 1227-1274. Italian scholastic philosopher, theologian, and writer.

Arnold, Matthew. 1822-1888. English poet and critic. One of his best-known poems is "Dover Beach" (1867).

Atahualpa. 1500?-1533. Last Inca king of Peru.

Atherton, Gertrude. 1857-1948. American novelist.

Bach, Richard [David]. 1936- . American editor and author. Best-known work is *Jonathan Livingstone Seagull* (1970).

Bacon, Lenice. 1895-1978. Quilt-collector and lecturer. Author of *American Patchwork Quilts* (1973).

Baldwin, James. 1924-1987. American novelist, playwright, and essayist. His work includes *Notes of a Native Son* (1955) and *Blues for Mister Charlie* (1964).

Balzac, Honoré de. 1799-1850. French novelist. His masterpiece is *La Comédie Humaine*, which fills 40 volumes and took 20 years to write.

Barfield, [Arthur] Owen. 1898- . English attorney, teacher and writer. Author of *Poetic Diction* (1929).

Baring-Gould, Sabine. 1834-1924. English author. His work includes the hymn "Onward Christian Soldiers" (1864).

Bede (Venerable Bede).673-735. English scholar, historian, and theologian.

Ben-Gurion, David. 1886-1973. Polish-born Israeli statesman.

Bergen, Candice. 1946- . American film actress.

Beston, Henry. 1888-1968. American naturalist and writer. Author of *The Outermost House: A Year of Life on the Great Beach of Cape Cod* (1928).

Biel, Gabriel. 1425?-1495. German scholastic philosopher.

Blake, Eubie [James Herbert]. 1883-1983. American ragtime musician and composer. His work includes the song, "I'm Just Wild About Harry" (1921).

Bok, Derek Curtis. 1930- . American lawyer and educator. 25th president of Harvard (1971).

Brillat-Savarin, Anthelme. 1755-1826. French politician and writer.

Bronte, Charlotte. 1816-1855. English novelist. Author of *Jane Eyre* (1847).

Browning, Robert. 1812-1889. English poet. Author of the epic poem, *The Ring and the Book*, (1864-1869).

Buson, Taniguchi. 1715-1783. Japanese poet.

Calderón de la Barca, Pedro. 1600-1681. Spanish dramatist and poet.

Camus, Albert. 1913-1960. Algerian-born French novelist, essayist, and playwright. Author of *The Stranger* (1942).

Carlyle, Thomas. 1795-1881. Scottish-born English historian, essayist, and philosopher. His most famous work is *The French Revolution* (1837).

Carman, [William] Bliss. 1861-1929. Canadian poet and journalist.

Carpenter, Liz [Elizabeth Sutherland]. 1920- . Newspaperwoman, author, and White House press secretary for Mrs. Lyndon Johnson (1963-1969).

Carter, Hodding. 1907-1972. American publisher, editor, writer, and crusader against racial intolerance.

Castaneda, Carlos Arana. 1931- . Brazilian-born American anthropologist. Author of *The Teachings of Don Juan, A Yaqui Way of Knowledge* (1968).

Cather, Willa [Sibert]. 1873-1947. American writer. Her work includes *My Antonia* (1918) and *Death Comes for the Archbishop* (1927).

Cervantes [Saavedra], Miguel de. 1547-1616. Spanish dramatist, poet, and novelist. Author of *El Ingeniosa Hidalgo Don Quixote de la Mancha* (1605, 1615).

Chamfort, Sebastien Roch Nicolas. 1741-1794. French writer and wit. Author of *Maximes*, published posthumously.

Channing, William Henry. 1810-1884. American Unitarian minister and social reformer.

Charlip, Remy. 1929- . American artist, poet, teacher, theatre director, and author.

Chaucer, Geoffrey. 1340?-1400. English soldier, government worker, public figure and poet. Author of *The Canterbury Tales* (started 1386).

Chesterfield, 4th Earl of. Philip Dormer Stanhope. 1694-1773. English statesman and man of letters.

Chesterton, G[ilbert] K[eith]. 1874-1936. English journalist and writer. His work includes the Father Brown detective stories (1911-1935).

Chicago, Judy. 1939- . American painter, writer, and lecturer. Her work includes *Embroidering Our Heritage: The Dinner Party Needlework* (1980).

Churchill, Sir Winston [Leonard Spencer]. 1874-1965. British statesman, biographer, and historian.

Coleridge, Samuel Taylor. 1772-1834. English poet and critic. His best-known work is *The Ancient Mariner* (1798).

Conant, James Bryant. 1893-1978. American educator, scientist, diplomat, and president of Harvard (1933-1953).

Confucius. c. 551-479 B.C. Chinese philosopher and teacher whose work is brought together in *The Analects*.

Coolidge, [John] Calvin. 1872-1933. Thirtieth president of the United States (1923-1929).

Cosby, Bill. 1937- . American comedian, actor, and writer.

Coudert, Jo. 1923- . American editor, copywriter, and author.

Craik, Dinah Maria Mulock. 1826-1887. English writer and poet. Author of *The Little Lame Prince* (1875).

Cullen, Countee. 1903-1946. American poet and writer.

Daly, Mary. 1928- . American educator, writer, and theologian.

Dickinson, Emily [Elizabeth]. 1830-1886. American poet. Author of 1,775 poems, only six of which were published in her lifetime.

Dylan, Bob. 1941- . American musician and songwriter.

Edison, Thomas Alva. 1847-1931. American inventor.

Einstein, Albert. 1879-1955. German-born, Swiss-educated American physicist. His work includes *The Meaning of Relativity* (1921).

Eliot, T[homas] S[tearns]. 1888-1965. American-born English poet, critic, and dramatist. Author of "Lovesong of J. Alfred Prufrock" (1915) and *Old Possum's Book of Practical Cats* (1939).

Elizabeth I. 1533-1603. Queen of England and Ireland (1558-1603).

Ellington, Duke [Edward Kennedy]. 1899-1974. American composer, and pianist. His work includes over 900 published pieces ranging from popular classics to sacred music, symphonic works, and incidental music for plays and motion pictures.

Emerson, Ralph Waldo. 1803-1882. American philosopher, essayist, lecturer, and poet. His work includes two volumes of *Essays* (1841-44], and *Poems* (1847).

Erasmus, Desiderius. 1466?-1536. Dutch scholar and philosopher.

Ertz, Susan. 1894-1985. English-born American novelist.

Farjeon, Eleanor. 1881-1965. English writer, especially known for her children's poetry.

Faulkner, William. 1897-1962. American novelist and short story writer. His work includes *Light in August* (1932).

Field, Eugene. 1850-1895. American journalist and poet, best known for his poems of childhood.

Fields, W[illiam] C[laude]. 1880-1946. American entertainer and film star.

Fitzgerald, Edward. 1809-1883. English poet and translator. Best known for his translation of the *Rubáiyát of Omar Khayyám* (1859).

Ford, Henry. 1863-1947. American machinist, businessman, and automobile manufacturer.

Francis of Assisi, Saint. c. 1181-1226. Italian friar and preacher, founder of the Franciscan order.

Franklin, Benjamin. 1706-1790. American statesman, scientist, inventor, philosopher, and writer. His work includes *Poor Richard's Almanac* (1732-1757).

Frost, Robert [Lee]. 1874-1963. American poet. His work includes *North of Boston* (1914).

Galileo Galilei. 1564-1642. Italian astronomer, physicist, and philosopher.

Gaskell, Mrs. [Elizabeth Cleghorn]. 1810-1865. English novelist. Author of *Cranford* (1853) and *Life of Charlotte Bronte* (1857).

Gautier, Théophile. 1811-1872. French poet, critic, and novelist.

Gibran, Kahlil. 1883-1931. Syrian-born American poet and artist. Author of *The Prophet* (1923).

Gilbert, Sir William [Schwenk]. 1836-1911. English playwright and collaborator with Arthur Sullivan in writing the Gilbert and Sullivan light operas (1875-1893).

Gill, Eric. 1882-1940. English sculptor, engraver, and type designer.

Goethe, Johann Wolfgang von. 1749-1832. German poet, dramatist, novelist, and philosopher. His best-known work is *Faust* (1808-1832).

Goldsmith, Oliver. 1728-1774. Irish-born English poet, playwright, and novelist. His work includes *The Vicar of Wakefield* (1766).

Grahame, Kenneth. 1859-1932. English banker and author. His best-known work is *The Wind in the Willows* (1908).

Gregory, Dick. 1932- . American comedian and civil rights activist.

Griffin, Susan. 1943- . American poet, writer, and educator. Her work includes *Made from this Earth* (1982).

Hale, Nancy. 1908- . American editor and writer. She is the author of *Mary Cassatt* (1975).

Haley, Alex [Palmer]. 1921- . American writer. Author of *Roots* (1976), which represents 12 years of research.

Hall, Eliza Calvert (pen name of Lida Calvert). 1856-1935. American writer and an activist in the woman's suffrage movement.

Hamilton, Anna E. 1843-1875. Irish poet.

Hammarskjold, Dag [Hjalmar Agne Carl]. 1905-1961. Swedish political economist. Secretary-General of the United Nations (1953-1961). Author of *Markings* (1964).

Harris, George Washington. 1814-1869. American humorist and newspaper columnist.

Harris, Sydney. 1917-1986. English-born American journalist, editor, and author. Best known for his "Strictly Personal" newspaper columns (1950-1983).

Hart, Moss. 1904-1961. American playwright and librettist. His work includes *The Man Who Came to Dinner* (1940).

Henri, Robert. 1865-1929. American painter. Author of *The Art Spirit* (1923).

Hepburn, Katharine. 1909- . American actress. Winner of four Academy Awards.

Heraclitus. c. 540?-480 B.C. Greek known as "The Weeping Philosopher."

Herbert, George. 1593-1633. English clergyman and poet. His work includes a collection of proverbs, *Jacula Prudentum* (1651).

Hesiod. Eighth century B.C. Greek poet. Author of *Works and Days.*

Hodgson, Ralph. 1871-1962. English poet.

Holmes, Oliver Wendell. 1809-1894. American physician anatomy professor, author, and man of letters. His work includes *The Autocrat of the Breakfast Table* (1858).

Horace [Quintus Horatius Flaccus]. 65-8 B.C. Roman lyric poet and satirist.

Hubbard, Elbert [Green]. 1856-1915. American businessman, writer, editor, and printer. Author of "A Message to Garcia" (1899).

Hunter, Alberta. 1895-1984. Blues singer and songwriter whose career spanned 70 years.

Huxley, Aldous [Leonard]. 1894-1963. English writer and critic. Author of *Brave New World* (1932).

Jackson, Helen Hunt. 1831-1885. American poet and novelist. Best known for *Ramona* (1884).

Jefferson, Thomas. 1743-1826. Third president of the United States (1801-1809), scholar, scientist, agriculturist, inventor, and architect.

Jewett, Sarah Orne. 1849-1909. American writer. Author of *The Country of the Pointed Firs* (1896).

Johnson, Samuel. 1709-1784. English poet, critic, and man of letters. His most famous work is his *Dictionary* (1747-1755).

Joseph, Jenny. 1932- . English poet and author. Her work includes several children's books.

Kanin, Garson. 1912- . American playwright, director, and author.

Keats, John. 1795-1821. English poet. Work includes "La Belle Dame Sans Merci" (1819).

Keillor, Garrison. 1942- . American humorist and writer. Author of *Lake Wobegon Days* (1985).

Keith, Sir Arthur. 1866-1955. Scottish-born English anthropologist.

Kent, Corita. 1918- . American graphic artist and social activist. Formerly a nun.

King, Martin Luther, Jr. 1929-1968. American minister, civil rights activist, and writer.

Kipling, Rudyard. 1865-1936. Indian-born English poet and writer. His work includes *The Jungle Books* (1894, 1895).

Korda, Michael Vincent. 1933- . American editor and author.

Lane, Rose Wilder. 1886-1968. American businesswoman, journalist, and writer. Author of *The Woman's Day Book of American Needlework* (1963).

Lawson, William. fl. 1618. English horticulturist. Author of *A New Orchard and Garden* (1618).

Lee, Ann [Mother]. 1736-1784. English-born mystic and religious leader. Founder of Shaker society in America (1776).

Le Gallienne, Richard. 1866-1947. English writer. His work includes *If I Were God* (1897).

Lincoln, Abraham. 1809-1865. Sixteenth president of the United States (1861-1865).

Lowell, James Russell. 1819-1891. American poet, essayist, and diplomat. His work includes, besides his books and poems, 50 anti-slavery articles written for contemporary periodicals.

Macaulay, Dame Rose. 1881-1958. English writer.

Macaulay, Thomas Babington. 1800-1859. English statesman, poet, historian, essayist, and biographer.

Marcus Aurelius [Antonius]. 121-180. Roman emperor (161-180) and stoic philosopher. Author of *Meditations*.

Markham, Edwin. 1852-1940. American poet best known for "The Man with the Hoe" (1899).

Masefield, John. 1878-1967. English playwright, poet, and author. Poet laureate (1930).

Mathews, William. 1819-1909. American author.

Mead, Margaret. 1901-1978. American anthropologist, writer, editor, and museum curator. Her work includes *Coming of Age in Samoa* (1928).

Melville, Herman. 1819-1891. American writer. Author of *Moby Dick* (1851).

Merton, Thomas. 1915-1968. French-born American priest, poet, essayist, and religious writer. Author of *The Seven Storey Mountain* (1948).

Mies Van der Rohe, Ludwig. 1886-1969. German-born American architect.

Milnes, Richard Monckton. 1809-1885. English statesman and poet.

Milton, John. 1608-1674. English poet. His work includes *Paradise Lost* (1667).

Mitchell, Margaret. 1900-1949. American novelist. Author of *Gone With the Wind* (1936).

More, Sir Thomas. 1478-1535. English statesman, author, and staunch supporter of Catholicism during the time of Henry VIII.

Moreau, Jeanne. 1928- . French film actress and director.

Morgan, Robin. 1941- . American poet, writer, and feminist. Editor of *Sisterhood Is Powerful* (1970).

Morley, Christopher. 1890-1957. American writer. His work includes *Kitty Foyle* (1939).

Muir, John. 1838-1914. Scottish-born naturalist, environmentalist, writer. Author of *Our National Parks* (1901).

Narihara. 825-880. Japanese poet.

Nash, Ogden. 1902-1971. American writer of humorous verse. His work includes *I'm a Stranger Here Myself* (1938).

Nearing, Scott. 1883-1983. American sociologist, lecturer, and political activist. Author, with Helen Nearing, of *Living the Good Life* (1954).

Newman, Cardinal John Henry. 1801-1890. English theologian, lecturer, and writer. Author of *Apologia pro Vita Sua* (1864).

Newton, John. 1725-1807. English clergyman and hymnwriter.

Niebuhr, Reinhold. 1892-1971. American clergyman, theologian, and writer. His work includes *Does Civilization Need Religion?* (1927).

Nietzsche, Friedrich [Wilhelm]. 1844-1900. German philosopher and poet.

Nizer, Louis. 1902- . American attorney, lecturer, and writer. Author of *My Life in Court* (1961).

Nouwen, Henri J[osef] M[achiel]. 1932- . Dutch-born Catholic priest, psychologist, and author. His work includes *The Wounded Healer: Ministry in Contemporary Society* (1972).

Omar Khayyám. ?-c. 1123. Persian poet and astronomer. Author of the Rubáiyát.

Ovid, [Publius Ovidus Naso]. 43 B.C.-?17 A.D. Roman poet. Work includes *Metamorphoses*.

Peale, Norman Vincent. 1898- . American clergyman and writer. Author of *The Power of Positive Thinking* (1952).

Persius [Aulus Persius Flaccus]. 34-62 A.D. Roman satirist.

Picasso, Pablo [Ruiz y]. 1881-1973. Spanish artist, prolific in nearly every mode of visual expression.

Plato. c. 428-348 B.C. Greek philosopher. Work includes *The Republic*.

Plautus, Titus Maccius. 254?-184 B.C. Umbrian-born Roman playwright.

Pliny the Younger. 61-105 A.D. Roman consul. Author of *Letters*.

Plutarch. 46?-120 A.D. Greek biographer. Author of *Parallel Lives*, studies in pairs of distinguished Greeks and Romans.

Pope, Alexander. 1688-1744. English poet and satirist. His work includes *Essay on Man* (1733).

Popeye. Cartoon character created by E.G. Segar in 1929.

Publilius Syrus. First century B.C. Latin playwright and actor.

Ray, John. 1627-1705. English naturalist. Best known for collection of proverbs (1670).

Rilke, Rainer Maria. 1875-1926. Prague-born German lyric poet and writer.

Robbins, Harold. 1916- . American novelist. His work includes *A Stone for Danny Fisher* (1952).

Rogers, Will[iam Penn Adair]. 1879-1935. American actor, lecturer, and humorist. His work includes *The Cowboy Philosopher on Prohibition* (1919).

Roosevelt, [Anna] Eleanor. 1884-1962. Lecturer, writer, social reformer, and humanitarian. Wife of 32nd president of the United States.

Rosten, Leo [Calvin]. 1908- . Polish-born American humorist, writer, political scientist, and teacher. His work includes *The Education of H*y*m*a*n* K*a*p*l*a*n** (1937).

Ruskin, John. 1819-1900. English art critic and social theorist. Author of *Stones of Venice* (1851-53).

Saadi, Muslih-uddin. 1184?-1291. Persian poet. Author of *Gulistan* (1258).

Sadat, Muhammad Anwar el. 1918-1981. Egyptian political leader.

Saint-Exupéry, Antoine de. 1900-1944. French aviator and writer. Author of *The Little Prince* (1943).

Saroyan, William. 1908-1981. American playwright and author. His work includes *My Name Is Aram* (1940).

Sarton, May. 1912- . Belgian-born American poet and writer. Her work in poetry, fiction, and autobiography, covering a span of over 50 years, includes *Plant Dreaming Deep* (1968) and *A World of Light* (1976).

Savile, Sir George. 1633-1695. English statesman, essayist, and one of the earliest writers of political pamphlets.

Savitch, Jessica. 1948-1983. American television newswoman and journalist. Author of *Anchorwoman* (1982).

Saxe, John Godfrey. 1816-1887. American editor and author of humorous verse.

Schiller, [Johann Christoph] Friedrich von. 1759-1805. German poet and playwright. Author of *Wilhelm Tell* (1804).

Schreiner, Olive. 1855-1920. South African novelist and essayist. Author of *Story of an African Farm* (1883).

Schweitzer, Albert. 1875-1965. French philosopher, theologian, musician, writer, and medical missionary.

Scott, Sir Walter. 1771-1832. Scottish poet, novelist, historian, and biographer. His work includes *Lady of the Lake* (1810) and *Ivanhoe* (1819).

Seattle, Chief. 1786?-1866. Indian chief, signed treaty (1855) ceding land to settlers. City of Seattle is named after him.

Seneca, Lucius Annaeus. 8 B.C.-65 A.D. Spanish-born Roman statesman, philosopher, playwright, and essayist. Tutor to Nero.

Shakespeare, William. 1564-1616. English dramatist and poet. Author of 36 plays including *Hamlet* (1600), *Macbeth* (1605), and *The Tempest* (1611).

Shaw, George Bernard. 1856-1950. Irish-born English novelist, critic, journalist, reformer, and dramatist. Author of *Pygmalion* (1913) and *Saint Joan* (1923).

Shelley, Percy Bysshe. 1792-1822. English poet. Work includes "Ode to the West Wind" (1819) and "To a Skylark" (1821).

Shoffstall, Veronica. 1952- . American poet.

Sidney, Sir Philip. 1554-1586. English poet, statesman, and soldier.

Smith, Sydney. 1771-1845. English clergyman, essayist, and one of the founders of the *Edinburgh Review* (1802).

Sora, Kawai. 1648-1710. Japanese poet.

Stevenson, Adlai [Ewing]. 1900-1965. American statesman and writer.

Swift, Jonathan. 1667-1745. Irish-born English satirist, political writer, poet, and clergyman. Author of *Gulliver's Travels* (1726).

Szold, Henrietta. 1860-1945. American Jewish Zionist leader. Founder and president (1912-1926) of Hadassah.

Taylor, Ann. 1782-1866. English children's poet. With sister Jane wrote *Hymns for Infant Minds* (1810).

Teasdale, Sara. 1884-1933. American poet. Work includes *Flame and Shadow* (1920).

Terence, [Publius Terentius Afer]. 185-159 B.C. Carthaginian-born Roman comic playwright.

Theroux, Paul [Edward]. 1941- . American novelist and travel writer. His work includes *The Kingdom by the Sea* (1983).

Thomas à Kempis. 1380-1471. German ecclesiastic and writer. Author of *Imitation of Christ* (c. 1420).

Thoreau, Henry David. 1817-1862. American essayist, philosopher, naturalist, and poet. His best-known work is *Walden, or Life in the Woods* (1854).

Trollope, Anthony. 1815-1882. English writer. His work includes the six volumes of "The Chronicles of Barsetshire" (1855-1867).

Twain, Mark. Pen name of Samuel Langhorne Clemens. 1835-1910. American humorist, newspaperman, lecturer, and writer. Author of *The Adventures of Tom Sawyer* (1876) and *The Adventures of Huckleberry Finn* (1884).

Vauvenargues, Luc de Clapiers. 1715-1747. French soldier and moralist. Author of *Réflexions et Maximes* (c. 1747).

Vinci, Leonardo da. 1452-1519. Italian painter, sculptor, architect, engineer, and scientist. Left behind a large body of manuscripts, drawings, and observations that were brought together after his death as *The Notebooks of Leonardo da Vinci.*

Walton, Izaak. 1593-1683. English biographer and writer. Author of *The Compleat Angler* (1653).

Washington, Martha [Dandridge Custis]. 1732-1802. Wife of first president of the United States.

Watts, Isaac. 1674-1748. English theologian, hymn-writer, and author. His work includes *Divine and Moral Songs for Children* (1720).

Webster, John. 1580?-?1625. English dramatist. Most famous play is *The Duchess of Malfi* (c. 1614).

Welty, Eudora. 1909- . American short story writer and novelist. She is the author of *One Writer's Beginnings* (1984).

Wesley, John. 1703-1791. Theologian, evangelist, and founder of Methodism. His work includes 23 collections of hymns.

Whipple, Henry Benjamin. 1822-1901. American Episcopal clergyman, first bishop of Minnesota (1859). Worked for reforms in Indian affairs.

Wilcox, Ella Wheeler. (1850-1919). American journalist and poet. Her best-known volume is *Poems of Passion* (1883).

Wilde, Oscar [Fingal O'Flahertie Wills]. 1854-1900. Irish wit, poet, and dramatist. Author of *The Importance of Being Earnest* (1895).

Winstanley, Gerrard. 1609-?1661. English Leveller (a political group advocating equality before the law, and religious toleration). Called the "Spiritual Father of the Quakers."

Wright, Charles. 1935- . American poet.

Wylie, Eleanor [Hoyt]. 1885-1928. American poet and novelist. Her work includes the collection *Nets to Catch the Wind* (1921).

Young, Edward. 1683-1765. English poet. Most famous work is *Night Thoughts* (1742-45).

Yuan Mei. 1715-1797. Chinese poet.

Acknowledgments

A special thank you to Odette Teel who lit the match, fanned the flames, and added a judicious log now and then; to Shirley Conlon who, as always, was unstintingly generous with knowledge and material; to Sydne Yanko-Jongbloed for supplying the missing links in my quilt library; to the San Pedro Regional Branch Library and its knowledgeable, patient, and unfailingly good-humored staff; to my sister Jeanne Gula, and friend Doris Miller for assistance with the always and ever last-minute details; to Stan Malotte, Matthew Miles, and Robert Miles, for keeping me literate; and, most especially, to the contributors without whom *Guiding Stars* never would have been at all.

All possible care has been taken to trace the copyright sources of material used in this book and to give full acknowledgment for its use. Any mistakes or omissions are unintentional, and we would appreciate being told of them that they may be corrected in future editions.

The editor and publishers gratefully acknowledge the permission granted by the following authors, publishers, and author's representatives to reprint some of their material in *Guiding Stars*.

Donna Abate: "May the world hug you today." Copyright © Blue Mountain Arts, Inc., 1984. All rights reserved. Reprinted by permission of Blue Mountain Arts, Boulder, CO.

Eden Ahbez: excerpt from the lyrics of "Nature Boy." Words and music copyright © 1948, renewed 1976 by Eden Ahbez. Reprinted by permission of the author.

Henry Beston: excerpt from *The Outermost House* by Henry Beston. Copyright © 1928, 1949, © 1956 by Henry Beston. Copyright © 1977 by Elizabeth C. Beston. Reprinted by permission of Henry Holt and Company, Inc., New York, NY.

The Holy Bible: Revised Standard Version. Copyright © 1971 by The Division of Christian Education, National Council of Churches of Christ in the United States of America.

Lena Bommelyn: quoted in "Northwest California Basketry" by Pam Mendelsohn, *Southwest Art*, June 1983 (Vol. 13, No. 1) page 59. Reprinted by permission of the editor.

Judy Chicago: excerpt from *Sisterhood Is Powerful*, edited by Robin Morgan. Copyright © 1970 by Robin Morgan. Published by Random House, Inc., New York, NY. Reprinted by permission of the publisher.

Flossie Cornett, Ethel Hall, Clemmie Pugh, and Lucy Stooksbury: quoted in *A People and Their Quilts* by John Rice Irwin, copyright © 1984 by John Rice Irwin. Published by Schiffer Publishing, Ltd., Exton, PA. Reprinted by permission of the author.

Countee Cullen: "Incident," from *On These I Stand.* Copyright © 1925 by Harper and Row, Publishers, Inc.,

New York, NY. Renewed 1953 by Ida M. Cullen. Reprinted by permission of Harper and Row, Publishers, Inc.

Mary Daly: excerpt from *Beyond God the Father* by Mary Daly. Copyright © 1973. Reprinted by permission of the publishers, Beacon Press, Boston, MA.

Robert Davidson: quotation from the cover of the book *Indian Artists at Work* by Ulli Steltzer, published by Douglas and McIntyre, Vancouver, BC, and Toronto, Ontario, copyright © 1976. Reprinted by permission of the publisher.

Fannie Stearns Davis: excerpt from "Souls" by Fannie Stearns Davis. Copyright © by Rebecca G. Lloyd. Reprinted by permission of Rebecca G. Lloyd.

Theo Eson: excerpt from "Grandma's Corner," *Quilter's Newsletter Magazine*, May 1978. Reprinted by permission of Leman Publications, Inc., Wheatridge, CO.

Eleanor Farjeon: "Morning Has Broken." Copyright © 1957 by Eleanor Farjeon. Reprinted by permission of Harold Ober Associates, Inc., New York, NY.

Robert Frost: excerpt from "Stopping by Woods on a Snowy Evening." Copyright 1923, © 1969 by Holt, Rinehart and Winston. Copyright © 1951 by Robert Frost. Reprinted from *The Poetry of Robert Frost* edited by Edward Connery Lathem, by permission of Henry Holt and Company, Inc., New York, NY.

Susan Griffin: excerpt from "To Gather Ourselves," from *Dear Sky* by Susan Griffin. Copyright © 1973 by Susan Griffin and Shameless Hussy Press, Berkeley, CA. Reprinted by permission of author and publisher.

Beth Gutcheon: excerpt from *The Quilt Design Workbook* by Beth and Jeffrey Gutcheon, published by Rawson Associates, Inc., New York, NY. Copyright © 1976 by Beth and Jeffrey Gutcheon. Reprinted by permission of Beth Gutcheon.

Isabelle Hooper Haight: "Spring's a soft coverlet," from *Machine Quilting for the Homemaker* by Ernest B. Haight, David City, NE. Copyright © 1974 by Ernest B. Haight. Reprinted by permission of Ernest B. Haight.

Dag Hammarskjold: excerpt from *Markings*, by Dag Hammarskjold, translated by Leif Sjoberg and W.H. Auden, copyright © 1964, by Alfred A. Knopf, Inc., New York, NY. Reprinted by permission of the publisher.

Jenny Joseph: "Warning," from *Rose in the Afternoon* by Jenny Joseph Dent, copyright © 1974 by Jenny Joseph. Reprinted by permission of John Johnson (Authors' Agent) Ltd., London.

Helen Kelley: excerpt from "Loose Threads," in *Quilter's Newsletter Magazine*, May 1983. Reprinted by permission of Leman Publications, Inc., Wheatridge, CO.

Rose Wilder Lane: excerpt from *Woman's Day Book of American Needlework* by Rose Wilder Lane. Copyright © 1961, 1962, 1963 by Fawcett Publications, Inc., NY. Reprinted by permission of the Woman's Day Resource Center, New York, NY.

Jean Ray Laury: excerpt from The *Creative Woman's Getting-It-All-Together-at-Home Handbook* by Jean Ray Laury. Copyright © 1977 by Litton Educational Publishing Inc. Reprinted by permission of the author.

Richard Le Gallienne: "I Meant to Do My Work Today," from *The Lonely Dancer and Other Poems* by Richard Le Gallienne. Copyright © 1913 by Dodd, Mead and Company. Copyright renewed 1941 by Richard Le Gallienne. Reprinted by permission of Dodd, Mead and Company, New York, NY.

Adelaide Love: "The Lien," from *The Slender Singing Tree* by Adelaide Love. Copyright © by Dodd, Mead and Company, Inc., New York, NY. Reprinted by permission of Dodd, Mead and Company, Inc.

Elise Maclay: "Carpenter," from *Green Winters — Celebrations of Old Age* by Elise Maclay, copyright © 1977 by Elise Maclay. Reprinted by permission of Reader's Digest Press, 200 Park Ave., New York, NY 10166.

Robin Morgan: excerpt from "Piecing," copyright © 1978 by Robin Morgan, from *Depth Perception* by Robin Morgan. Reprinted by permission of Doubleday and Company, Inc., New York, NY.

Ogden Nash: "The Ant." From *Verses from 1929 On* by Ogden Nash. Copyright © 1935 by Ogden Nash. Reprinted by permission of Little, Brown and Company, Boston, MA.

Henri Nouwen: quotation on friendship. Reprinted by permission of Henry J.M. Nouwen, Daybreak, Richmond Hill, Ontario.

Progressive Farmer: excerpt from July, 1973. Reprinted by permission of the *Progressive Farmer*, Birmingham, AL.

Rainier Maria Rilke: excerpt from *Letters to a Young Poet* (#4), translated by M. D. Herter Norton, by permission of W. W. Norton and Company, Inc. Copyright © 1934 by W. W. Norton and Company, Inc., New York and London. Renewed 1962 by M. D. Herter Norton. Reprinted by permission of the publisher.

Harold Robbins: excerpt from *The Inheritors* by Harold Robbins. Copyright © 1969 by Harold Robbins. Reprinted by permission of Simon and Schuster, New York, NY.

Leo Rosten: excerpt from *Captain Newman, M.D.* by Leo Rosten. Copyright © 1956, 1958, 1961 by Leo Rosten. Reprinted by permission of the author.

Antoine de Saint-Exupéry: excerpt from *The Little Prince* by Antoine de Saint-Exupéry, copyright © 1943, 1971 by Harcourt Brace Jovanovich, Inc., Orlando, FL. Reprinted by permission of the publisher.

William Saroyan: excerpt from *The Time of Your Life*,

copyright © 1939 by Harcourt, Brace and Company. Copyright © 1987 by the William Saroyan Foundation, San Francisco, CA. Reprinted by permission of the William Saroyan Foundation.

May Sarton: excerpts from *Mrs. Stevens Hears the Mermaids Singing*, copyright © 1965 by May Sarton; *Journal of a Solitude* by May Sarton, copyright © 1973 by May Sarton; "A Flower-Arranging Summer" and "Italian Garden" from *Selected Poems of May Sarton*, edited by Serena Sue Hilsinger and Lois Byrnes, copyright © 1978 by May Sarton; and *Recovering* by May Sarton, copyright © 1980 by May Sarton. All published by W. W. Norton and Company, New York/London. Reprinted by permission of the author.

Toby D. Schwartz: "On One's Own Room," from *Mercy Lord! My Husband's in the Kitchen* by Toby D. Schwartz. Copyright © 1981 by Toby Devens Schwartz. Reprinted by permission of Doubleday and Company, New York, NY.

Shoffstall, Veronica: "After a While." Copyright © 1971 by Veronica Shoffstall. Reprinted by permission of the author.

Jeannie Spears: excerpt from *The Professional Quilter*, July, 1984, The Oliver Press, St. Paul, MN. Reprinted by permission of Jeannie Spears.

Sara Teasdale: excerpt from "Barter." Reprinted by permission of Macmillan Publishing Company, New York, NY, from "Barter," by Sara Teasdale. Copyright © 1917 by Macmillan Publishing Company, renewed 1945 by Mamie T. Wheless.

Paul Theroux: excerpt from *The Old Patagonian Express* by Paul Theroux. Copyright © 1979 by Cape Cod Scriveners Company. Reprinted by permission of Houghton Mifflin Company, Boston, MA.

Anne Truitt: excerpts from *Daybook: The Journal of an Artist* by Anne Truitt. Copyright © 1982. Reprinted by permission of Houghton Mifflin Company, Boston, MA.

Charles Wright: excerpt from "The Other Side of the River" by Charles Wright. Reprinted by permission; copyright © 1982 by Charles Wright. Originally in *The New Yorker*.

Eleanor Wylie: two verses from "Let No Charitable Hope," from *Collected Poems of Eleanor Wylie*. Copyright © 1932 by Alfred A. Knopf, Inc., New York, NY, and renewed 1960 by Edwina C. Rubenstein. Reprinted by permission of the publisher.

Sōetsu Yanagi: excerpt from *The Unknown Craftsman* by Sōetsu Yanagi, with permission from Kodansha International, New York, NY, copyright © 1972.

Some of the contributors' own words in the biographical entries first appeared elsewhere. We wish to make acknowledgment and express our appreciation to those authors and publishers who have allowed us to reprint the quotations here.

Norma Bradley Allen, Carol Crabb, Sheila Groman, Beth Gutcheon, Helen Kelley, Joanne Kost, Bonnie Leonard, Ione McIntyre, Linda Platt, Jeannie M. Spears, and Susan Turbak: all reprinted from various issues of *Quilter's Newsletter Magazine*, a publication of Leman Publications, Inc., Wheatridge, CO, by permission.

Jinny Beyer: reprinted from *The Quilter's Album of Blocks and Borders*, EPM Publications, Inc., McLean, VA, copyright © 1980 by Jinny Beyer.

Helen Bitar: reprinted from *The Creative Woman's Getting-It-All-Together-at-Home Handbook*, by Jean Ray Laury. Copyright © 1977 by Litton Educational Publishing, Inc.

Karey Bresenhan: reprinted from *Hands All Around: Quilts from Many Nations* by Robert Bishop, Karey B. Bresenhan, and Bonnie Leman. Copyright © 1987 by E. P. Dutton, Inc., New York, NY.

Margaret Cavigga: reprinted from "Quilts: Stitching Layers of History, by Virginia Gray, *Los Angeles Times Home Section*, November 27, 1983.

Katy Christopherson, Joe Cunningham, Jean Mitchell, and Mary Schafer: reprinted from *Lady's Circle Patchwork Quilts*, published by Lopez Publications, Inc., New York, NY.

Barbara Crane, Dorothy Finley, Mildred Locke, Patricia Morris, and Julia Needham: reprinted from *American Quilter*, published by the American Quilter's Society, Division of Schroeder Publishing Company, Inc., Paducah, KY.

Cindy Vermillion Davis: reprinted from *Quilters' Journal* #21, by permission of Joyce Gross, publisher and editor, Mill Valley, CA.

Elly Dyson: reprinted from *America's Pictorial Quilts* by Caron L. Mosey, published by American Quilter's Society, Paducah, KY. Copyright © 1985 by Caron L. Mosey.

Margit Echols: reprinted from *The New American Quilt.* Copyright © by Margit Echols, Rowhouse Press, Box 20531, Cathedral Finance Station, New York, NY.

Jean Eitel: from *Quilt;* and John Mangiapane: from *Quilt Almanac;* both published by Harris Publications, Inc., New York, NY.

Mary Golden: reprinted from *The Friendship Quilt Book* by Mary Golden. Copyright © 1985 by Yankee Publishing, Inc., Dublin, NH. By permission of the publisher.

Genevieve Guracar (bulbul): cartoon, "If we can risk nuclear war, we can risk disarmament." Copyright © 1982 bulbul, Arachne Publishing, Mountain View, CA. Reprinted by permission of the artist.

Jan Halgrimson: reprinted from *Great Scrap Bag Quilts*, Weaver-Finch Publications, Edmonds, WA. Copyright © 1980 by Jan Halgrimson.

Carla Hassel: reprinted from *Super Quilter II*, Wallace-Homestead Book Company, Des Moines IA. Copyright © 1982 by Carla Hassel.

Dixie Haywood, Margaret Horton, and Helen Scott: reprinted from *Quilt World;* Hazel Carter and Jean Dubois: from *Quilt World Omnibook;* and Kathy Munkelwitz and Vivian Ritter: from *Stitch 'n Sew Quilts*, all published by The House of White Birches, Inc., Berne, IN.

Doris Hoover: reprinted from *The Third, and Last, Free Open Chain Annual*, copyright © 1983, Fibar Designs, with permission from Robbie Fanning, P.O. Box 2634, Menlo Park, CA 94026.

Roberta Horton: reprinted from *Calico and Beyond*, C & T Publishing, Lafayette, CA, copyright © 1986 by Roberta Horton.

John Rice Irwin: reprinted from *A People and Their Quilts*, Schiffer Publishing, Ltd., Exton, PA, copyright © 1984 by John Rice Irwin.

Michael James: reprinted from "Surviving Without Selling Out," from *The Quilt Digest*, Kiracofe and Kile, San Francisco, CA, copyright © 1983 by Kiracofe and Kile.

Jean Johnson: reprinted from *The Professional Quilter*, May 1985. Published by the Oliver Press, St. Paul, MN.

Yvonne Khin: reprinted from *The Collector's Dictionary of Quilt Names and Patterns*, Acropolis Books, Ltd., Washington, D.C. Copyright © 1980 by Yvonne Khin.

Bee Neeley Kuckelman: reprinted from "Starry, Starry Quilt," from *Keep Me in Stitches*, copyright © 1985 by Bee Neeley Kuckelman.

Jean Ray Laury: reprinted from *The Creative Woman's Getting-It-All-Together-At-Home Handbook*, by Jean Ray Laury. Copyright © 1977 by Litton Educational Publishing, Inc., New York, NY.

Millie Leathers: reprinted from *First, Nine and Always*, published by American Quilter's Society, Paducah, KY. Copyright © 1986 by Millie Leathers.

Diana Leone: reprinted from *The Sampler Quilt*, Leone Publications, Santa Clara, CA. Copyright © 1980 by Diana Leone.

Marsha McCloskey: reprinted from *Wall Quilts*, copyright © 1983 by Marsha Reynolds McCloskey. Published by That Patchwork Place, Inc., P.O. Box 118, Bothell, WA 98041.

Cyril Nelson: reprinted from *The Quilt Engagement Calendar, 1977*, compiled by Cyril I. Nelson, copyright © 1976 by E.P. Dutton, Inc., New York, NY.

Charlotte Patera: reprinted from Better Homes and Gardens *Applique Book by Charlotte Patera*, copyright © 1974 by Meredith Corporation, Des Moines, IA. All rights reserved.

Judy Rehmel: *Key to 1000 Quilt Patterns*. Copyright © 1978 by Judy Rehmel.

Penny Rigdon: reprinted from "About Quilts," *embroiderer's journal*, July 1973, copyright © 1973 by Handweaver and Craftsman, Inc., New York, NY.

Judy Robbins: reprinted from *The Ribbon* with permission from Lark Books, 50 College St., Asheville, NC 28801.

Elly Sienkiewicz: reprinted from *Spoken Without a Word* by Elly Sienkiewicz, copyright © 1983 by The Turtle Hill Press, Washington, D. C.

Ami Simms: reprinted from "How to Outwit Your Quilt," from *Quilt Almanac*, 1986; and *Little Ditties*, copyright © 1986 by Ami Simms.

Judy Tomlonson: reprinted from *Mennonite Quilts and Pieces* by Judy Tomlonson, copyright © 1985 by Good Books, Intercourse, PA 17534.

Nan Tournier: reprinted from *First Prize Quilts*, Simon and Schuster, New York, NY, copyright © 1984 by Dimetra Makris.

Index

Authors' names are in italics, contributors' names are in roman.

Kanin, Garson, 20, 252
Keats, John, 23, 252
Keillor, Garrison, 38, 132, 252
Keith, Sir Arthur, 72, 253

Editor Elaine Miles lives in San Pedro, California with her husband and seven cats.